Real Project Leadership

# Real Project Leadership

The proven recipe for project
teams to have real impact

JEANETTE CREMOR

NATIONAL
LIBRARY
OF AUSTRALIA

A catalogue record for this
book is available from the
National Library of Australia

# Acknowledgements

To my daughter, Kirsty, and granddaughter, Willow, you are my purpose and inspiration. My most precious gift is exploring life and creating moments with you. Dream big, you are enough, and it is all possible.

They say people come into your life for a reason, a season or a lifetime. To my forever besties in Queensland and Victoria, thank you for always being beside me on the good and bad days.

To the many project teams I have worked with, what a ride it was. Thank you for pushing me, teaching me and supporting me.

To my project career role models – Dana, Sam, Mike and Alex. I was blessed to be in the room with you. I listened to and watched your every word, behaviour and action. You filled my cup to be a better project leader.

To my clients, thank you for the opportunity to be part of your transformation journeys. We've had tough conversations and celebrated wins. I have lost count of the number of sticky notes and chocolates consumed in our workshops.

We don't get far along the path of our work and life journeys without mentors and coaches. To Janine and Jane, thank you for holding the space for me to develop my thought leadership, establish my practice, and put pen to paper to write this book. Your guidance and gentle butt kicks have all been offered with no judgement. Forever grateful.

# Contents

Introduction: The Challenges Ahead of Us                1

    Project teams are struggling                        7

    My curiosity for real project leadership            11

The Proven Recipe                                       15

    A framework for business transformation journeys    16

    From unaware to trust                               18

    Five additional points to consider                  23

## PILLAR 1: Self Leadership

Ingredient #1: Self-awareness                           29

Ingredient #2: Values and principles                    35

Ingredient #3: Growth mindset                           41

Ingredient #4: Resilience                               47

Ingredient #5: Self-discipline                          53

Self Leadership Reflection                              57

Self Leadership Checklist                               58

# PILLAR 2: Solution Leadership

Ingredient #6: Critical thinking     63

Ingredient #7: Innovation     69

Ingredient #8: Adaptability     75

Ingredient #9: Problem solving     81

Ingredient #10: Risk management     87

Solution Leadership Reflection     92

Solution Leadership Checklist     93

# PILLAR 3: Practice Leadership

Ingredient #11: Decision making     99

Ingredient #12: Team building     107

Ingredient #13: Communication     117

Ingredient #14: Delegation     125

Ingredient #15: Performance management     133

Practice Leadership Reflection     141

Practice Leadership Checklist     143

The Secret Sauce for Lasting Success     145

    Role model     147

    Team legacy     150

References     155

About Jeanette     157

# INTRODUCTION

# The Challenges Ahead of Us

Andrea, freshly elevated to a leadership position, was thrown into a challenging scenario: steering a newly formed project team that was unacquainted with the organisational context and culture. The team, while competent, was navigating blindly without a compass of cultural norms, values and historical insights into decision-making processes within the organisation. Andrea recognised that this disconnect could breed misalignments and misunderstandings, potentially derailing the project.

Henry, meanwhile, encountered a storm as he faced continuous churn within his project team, disrupting workflow and causing inefficiencies. Digging deeper, he discovered work-life balance struggles and a visible absence of recognition, leading to resentment among his team members.

Lily, embroiled in an ongoing battle against timelines, with her project team invariably falling behind, was stuck in a predicament that threatened the project's viability. The puzzle was multifaceted: detecting whether the issue stemmed from inadequate planning, resource constraints, or inefficiencies within the team's way of working.

These are just some of the challenges faced by people leaders and their project teams, as they navigate the complexity of business transformations in rapid change cycles.

To understand how much change has occurred – and the challenges this presents – let's take a step back in time...

The **1970s** saw the introduction of personal computers, which began permeating through businesses and later, homes. We also saw the ignition of social and environmental movements such as Earth Day towards more equitable and sustainable practices.

In the **1980s**, we witnessed computers becoming more commonplace, and the seeds of the internet were sown. Meanwhile, environmental conversations were getting louder, bringing environmental considerations into policy and industrial practice.

The **1990s** embraced global trade and integrated markets. The digital age found its true awakening with the advent of the World Wide Web, transitioning us into an unprecedented era of connectivity and information exchange.

The **2000s** surged in technology advancements with the increasing accessibility and influence of the internet, as well as mobile technologies and social media platforms. We also saw a gradual shift in tangible actions around sustainability, climate change and corporate social responsibility.

The **2010s** brought advanced technologies – like artificial intelligence (AI), the internet of things, and blockchain – to entire industries, economies, and even daily life. The urgency to address environmental challenges also intensified, through international accords and grassroots movements.

So, what change and challenges are in front of us in the 2020s and beyond?

The business world will continue to transform, marked by rapid technological advancements, globalisation, and evolving customer expectations.

# Technological revolution

The advent of AI, machine learning and blockchain is not just a trend but a seismic shift in how businesses operate. Organisations worldwide are grappling with integrating these technologies into their operations. This technological revolution demands not only technical acumen but also strategic vision from project leaders.

# Globalisation and market diversity

As businesses extend their reach globally, they encounter diverse markets and regulatory environments. This expansion is not merely geographic but also cultural, demanding project leaders who are not only adept at managing logistical complexities but also skilled in cultural intelligence.

# Shifting customer expectations

Today's customers are more informed and demanding. They seek personalised, high-quality products and services, compelling organisations to consistently innovate and elevate their offerings.

## Competitive pressures and the need for agility

In a world where change is the only constant, agility becomes a cornerstone for survival and success. High-performing project teams are at the forefront, driving innovation and ensuring organisational resilience in the face of change.

## Embracing sustainability and social responsibility

Projects today are often infused with elements of sustainability and social responsibility. Leaders must align projects not only with business goals but also with broader societal and environmental objectives.

## The talent conundrum

The talent shortage, skills gap and evolving employee expectations present a unique challenge. Leaders must cultivate teams that are not only skilled but also aligned with the organisation's values and foster a culture of continuous learning and adaptation.

## The critical role of senior accountable officers

In a world that's more interconnected than ever, these challenges have a ripple effect on the global economy and society. Effective project leadership is not just about steering projects to completion but also about driving innovation and sustainable growth that resonates on a global scale.

The senior accountable officers are the navigators in this complex landscape. Their decisions and leadership styles have a profound impact on the direction and success of projects.

Their role entails a significant responsibility: to lead teams effectively, foster innovation, and ensure projects align with both organisational goals and broader societal values. They are not just managing teams; they are shaping the future of their organisations and, by extension, the industries they operate in.

In the Future of Jobs Report 2023,[1] the World Economic Forum states:

> 'Over 85% of organisations surveyed identify increased adoption of new and frontier technologies and broadening digital access as the trends most likely to drive transformation in their organisation. Broader application of Environmental, Social and Governance (ESG) standards within their organisations will also have a significant impact.'

Meanwhile, a 2023 *Harvard Business Review* article,[2] by Deborah Perry Piscione and Josh Drean, outlines the forces that are fundamentally changing how we work:

> 'The traditional boundaries of work that have confined many of us – cubicles, set schedules, and geographic limitations, to name a few – have essentially been shattered by the pandemic,

*by forces of globalisation, and by the rising gig economy, all while work is being augmented by Web3 and generative AI (GenAI) technologies. These seismic shifts are fuelling a new work model — a 24/7, boundaryless ecosystem of collaboration that spans continents, time zones, and cultures.'*

In these dynamic business environments, focusing on new ways of working, new capabilities and new technologies is the only way forward for organisations.

Organisations must have high-performing project teams as the engine driving business transformation in value creation. In other words, boosting overall performance through increased revenue, lower operating costs, and better customer satisfaction and workforce productivity.

A 2022 Gartner survey of nearly 3,500 employees found that when organisations help employees build connections intentionally, their employees are five times as likely to be on a high-performing team and twelve times as likely to feel connected to their colleagues.[3]

So, what does all this mean for the people leaders accountable for project teams and the results they deliver?

Worryingly, research shows that despite the crucial role project teams play, they're struggling to perform at their best.

# Project teams are struggling

A report titled 'The State of Project Management in Australia 2022', produced by KPMG and the Australian Institute of Project Management (AIPM), revealed a number of key findings:

- Project professionals with exceptional interpersonal skills will be the leaders of the future.

- Strong leadership and relationships are as important as technical know-how.

- Project professionals and organisations must evolve to thrive in complexity.

However, the report – which is based on a survey of 329 Australian project professionals – went on to identify a number of worrying statistics, including the following:

- 42% said their organisation wasn't doing anything (or they didn't know what they were doing) to attract and encourage emerging project professionals.

- 39% said team stress and burnout were increasing.

- 48% said their projects were delivered with stakeholder satisfaction most of the time, compared to 52% in 2020.

- 36% said their projects were delivered on-budget most of the time, compared to 40% in 2020.

- 32% said their projects were delivered on time most of the time, compared to 42% in 2020.

- 43% of respondents feel their organisation manages projects and programs effectively or very effectively, compared to 48% in 2020.

*'The perception of effective management of projects has slipped compared to 2020, and so have most success metrics,'* the report states.

I have witnessed the problems firsthand, overseeing countless project journeys as a project coordinator, business analyst, project manager, PMO manager and program director.

In more recent discussions with senior responsible officers, general managers and directors, I've heard their stories about the recurring challenges in team management, strategic alignment and operational efficiency. Here are some of the organisational issues they are grappling with:

- **Managing team dynamics and conflicts**

  In any organisation, fostering a harmonious and collaborative team environment is crucial yet challenging. This becomes particularly complex in large or cross-functional teams, where diversity in professional backgrounds and perspectives can lead to friction. Each team member brings unique experiences, work styles and thought processes, which, while enriching the team's capabilities, can also lead to misunderstandings and conflicts. The leadership's role involves recognising and valuing these differences, facilitating open communication, and establishing a common ground where diverse opinions are respected and integrated. Conflict resolution strategies become essential, where the focus is not only on addressing immediate disagreements but also on building a foundation for proactive, constructive conversations. In essence, managing team dynamics is about creating an environment where diverse talents synergise rather than collide.

- **Aligning operations with strategic objectives**

  An organisation's operations are the gears that turn the wheels of its strategic vision. The challenge lies in ensuring that these operations are not just efficient day-to-day activities but also stepping stones towards long-term strategic goals. This alignment requires a deep understanding of the organisation's vision and the ability to translate this vision into actionable plans. Leaders must effectively communicate the 'big picture', helping team members understand how their roles contribute to broader objectives. It involves setting clear, measurable goals, and aligning resources, processes and initiatives in a way that they collectively drive the strategic agenda. This alignment is not a one-time effort but a continuous process of adaptation and realignment as both operational capabilities and strategic objectives evolve.

- **Managing change**

  Change is a constant in the business landscape, yet it remains one of the most challenging aspects to manage. Whether it's a minor process adjustment or a major strategic shift, change often breeds resistance and uncertainty. Employees may fear the unknown or feel comfortable with the status quo, making it difficult to embrace change. Effective change management involves clear communication, where the reasons for change, the expected outcomes, and the steps involved are transparently conveyed. It also requires empathetic leadership – acknowledging concerns, providing support, and involving team members in the change process. Training and development initiatives are often critical to equip teams with the skills and knowledge needed to navigate new systems or processes. Ultimately, managing change is about creating a culture where change is viewed not as a disruption but as an opportunity for growth and improvement.

- **Balancing short-term and long-term priorities**

  Organisations often find themselves walking a tightrope between addressing immediate operational needs and pursuing long-term strategic objectives. This balancing act is intricate, as focusing too much on short-term tasks can derail long-term goals, while an excessive long-term focus may lead to current operational inefficiencies or missed opportunities. Effective leadership requires a dual lens: operational excellence to meet current demands and strategic foresight to pave the way for future success. This involves prioritising and sequencing activities, making informed trade-offs and maintaining agility to adapt as priorities shift. It also requires a clear communication strategy, where team members understand both the immediate tasks at hand and the future vision they are working towards.

- **Boosting team performance and productivity**

  Enhancing team performance and productivity is an ongoing challenge in any organisation. It requires a multifaceted approach: setting clear goals and expectations, providing the necessary tools and resources, fostering a motivating work environment, and continuously monitoring and providing feedback on performance. Leadership plays a crucial role in identifying and leveraging the strengths of each team member, fostering a culture of continuous improvement and learning. Recognition and rewards are important to keep morale high, but equally important are development opportunities that allow team members to grow and advance. Productivity also hinges on efficient processes and workflows, which should be regularly reviewed and optimised. The goal is to create a team that is not just high-performing but also adaptable, collaborative, and aligned with the organisation's vision and values.

So, is there a way to address these challenges? The answer is yes. As an experienced project and change leader, I believe the key is *real project leadership*.

# My curiosity for real project leadership

With my first taste of projects, I was addicted.

In my twenties as a contract administrator, sitting with road construction engineers listening and watching, I was intrigued and wanted to know more about projects — I was hooked. I dipped my toe into the project arena, learning about structure, schedules, budgets, issues and documentation.

It was when I stepped into the world of technology, ten years later as a procurement specialist, that I had eye-opening experiences about people. The people I worked with, the people I worked for, the people I was impacting ... and that together they made a difference in project success or failure. So when the opportunity arose to learn about change management and building teams, I jumped at it. That kickstarted my project career.

For twenty years, while I led or recovered large complex projects integrating people, process and technology, I educated myself, observed team dynamics, analysed performance, assessed research, tested new things, and developed a recipe for high-performing project teams who deliver extraordinary results.

Yet the time spent in the sports industry, specifically with AFL, swimming and cycling professional athletes, has been my greatest classroom when it comes to project team success. The light bulb moment – which tested my perspective of what shapes team success – was when I found myself in the back of a room listening to Leigh Matthews, then head coach of the Brisbane Lions AFL Club. He shared his wisdom about team strategy, execution and performance. My curiosity amplified. How could his philosophy of 'everyone has a role to play' be applied in project team environments?

In 2017, I developed The Project Ecosystem®, a planning and delivery framework for business transformation journeys, from strategy to operations. In this book, I share with you the ingredients from my proven recipe for real project leadership, the core component of the framework.

This is a practical, 'when I need it' book. Read a couple of pages and reflect. Jot down some ideas, pick one and take action. I hope that, after several months and years, this book looks tired and well used, full of notes and highlighter marks.

Let's get real.

# The Proven Recipe

Real Project Leadership is about behaviours and actions, not titles, and everyone has a role to play.

When a project team collectively demonstrates real project leadership through their behaviours and actions, they have real impact — by having confidence in their project role as a collaborator; building trusted relationships with stakeholders who feel valued; and thriving as an empowered, high-performing team believing anything is possible.

When each member of a project team is trusted to fulfil their respective role, it resembles the harmonious orchestration of an Olympic eight-person rowing team. Each rower, powerful and proficient, contributes to the collective rhythm, pulling their oars in synchronised unity. Their eyes are on the coxswain, trusting their guidance. Each stroke, each adjustment, mirrors the tactical decisions made during a project. Their unwavering focus is on what lies ahead, towards the finish line — the coveted project completion.

As the boat cuts through the water, gliding swiftly and smoothly, it manifests the shared vision of the team, their collective drive propelling them towards success. Their journey encapsulates trust, collaboration and shared triumph — the very essence of real project leadership. The finish line is not just a destination but a celebration of a shared success story.

# A framework for business transformation journeys

As highlighted in the Introduction, business transformation journeys are becoming more complex, with many moving parts. When an eye is taken off one of the key project activities, things can start to unravel. If no action is taken, the project will not deliver the expected benefits or will ultimately fail.

A 2023 article published by CIO.com[4] states, *'Despite strategic alignment among IT and business leaders, technical and transformational initiatives still fall flat at an unacceptable rate.'* The article goes on to list some of the common causes, including:

- Little or no executive support.
- Lack of business sponsor engagement and accountability.
- Not enough resources or not the right ones.
- Lack of collaboration.

The Project Ecosystem®

Earlier I mentioned that in 2017, based on hundreds of hours of interviews and research, and unpacking all of my own project case studies, I developed The Project Ecosystem® – a planning and delivery framework for business transformation journeys.

All thirteen inter-related components, shown in the diagram, work together to support the right project, with the right team, at the right time. At the core is real project leadership – the collective behaviours and actions of a project team to achieve real impact.

Here's a quick overview of what I mean by 'real impact':

**Real Project Leadership = Real Impact**

When you are facilitating a workshop,
you are leading the room.

When you are having a conversation,
you are leading the headlines.

When you are testing a system, you are leading the results.

When you are considering feedback, you
are leading the improvement.

When you are transparent, you are leading the trust.

When you are actively listening, you are leading the empathy.

When you are sharing knowledge, you
are leading the learning curve.

# From unaware to trust

Imagine stepping into a bustling conference for the first time, a world teeming with potential connections, insights and learning. This experience, much like venturing into a room filled with strangers, carries an air of the unknown, an uncharted territory of possibilities. Initially, there's an unmistakable feeling of uncertainty – a cocktail of anticipation and apprehension. The room buzzes with the sounds of introductions and the exchange of ideas.

In these early moments, you're an observer on the periphery, trying to soak in the new environment. Who do you approach? What conversations do you join? The faces in the crowd are just that, faces, not yet acquaintances or colleagues. This initial phase of uncertainty mirrors the beginning stages of many new experiences – unfamiliar yet brimming with potential. The challenge and opportunity lie in stepping forward, initiating conversations, and transforming the unknown faces into valuable connections and the uncertainty into a path of learning and growth. Just as in any new project or team setting, the initial unease gradually gives way to familiarity and confidence as you find your bearings and begin to engage with the vibrant world around you.

The Real Project Leadership (RPL) six level model serves as an insightful tool for project teams to assess and guide their development in project environments. It emphasises the importance of not just the tasks at hand (activity), but also how individuals approach these tasks (behaviour) and the effectiveness of their contributions (delivery). This holistic view encourages a more comprehensive approach to personal and project team development from the basic level of engagement and understanding to a stage where trust and high performance defines leadership excellence.

|  | Team Activity | Team Behaviour | Team Results |
|---|---|---|---|
| 6 | Trust | Performing | 150% |
| 5 | Impact | Innovating | 100% |
| 4 | Visible | Engaging | 80% |
| 3 | Instruct | Leading | 50% |
| 2 | Invisible | Responding | 20% |
| 1 | Unaware | Questioning | 0% |

**Level 1 – Unaware:** Project team members are not aware of their responsibilities or the overall goals of the project. They are largely reactive, constantly questioning what needs to be done instead of being proactive. They contribute little to the project's overall progress.

The project team needs to understand their role better and start participating actively in the project, focusing on learning, self-development, and understanding the bigger picture.

*Key actions:* Foster a culture of open communication and learning. Team members should be encouraged to ask questions and get clarifying information to perform their roles. Feedback should focus on strengthening understanding and enhancing self-awareness.

**Level 2 – Invisible:** Project team members are responding to tasks given, but do not initiate or lead any project activities. Their contribution is passive and largely unnoticed, but their work is necessary for the project.

The project team needs to be more proactive, show initiative, and participate in decision-making processes.

**Key actions:** Recognise timely responses to tasks. Provide constructive feedback on how team members can take initiative and enhance their involvement in project activities. Celebrate when a team member takes initiative or handles a task proactively, showing a growth mindset.

**Level 3 – Instruct:** Project team members start taking a leadership role within their responsibilities, giving instructions, and driving progress in their area. Their behaviour is starting to have an effect on the project's outcomes.

The project team needs to start communicating more effectively, engaging with others, and making their work more visible to move up the scale.

**Key actions:** Observe how well team members are adapting to specific roles, providing feedback on their leadership skills and decision-making abilities. It's essential to celebrate milestones achieved under their responsibility, further encouraging them to lead.

**Level 4 – Visible:** Project team members have a more active role in the team. The team member is now visibly contributing to the project, engaging with others, and having a significant impact on the project's progress. They are a critical component in the project's success.

The project team should focus on innovative solutions and strategies, and on broadening their impact across the entire project.

*Key actions:* Focus on how effectively team members engage with others and contribute to the project visibly. Feedback should centre on their teamwork, communication skills, and overall contribution to the project. Celebrate when a team member successfully facilitates a solution or achieves a goal that required significant collaboration.

**Level 5 – Impact:** Project team members are making a significant impact on the project. They are innovative, regularly offering new ideas, and leading efforts to improve the project's efficiency and effectiveness.

The project team should maintain a high level of performance, and earn the trust of their team and stakeholders.

*Key actions:* Observe the innovative ideas and strategies that team members are bringing to the project. Feedback should emphasise their creativity, problem-solving skills, and ability to drive change. Celebrations can be held for successful implementation of an innovative solution or notable improvement in project efficiency.

**Level 6 – Trust:** Project team members are trusted implicitly by all stakeholders. They consistently deliver excellent results, often exceeding expectations.

The project team should maintain this level of trust and performance, as well as mentoring others to uplift organisation capabilities. The importance of trust cannot be overstated. A 2017 *Harvard Business Review* article,[5] titled 'The Neuroscience of Trust', states, *'Compared with people at low-trust companies, people at high-trust companies report:*

*74% less stress, 106% more energy at work, 50% higher productivity, 13% fewer sick days, 76% more engagement, 29% more satisfaction with their lives, and 40% less burnout.'*

**Key actions:** Observe how consistently team members are performing and whether they're maintaining the trust they've earned. Feedback should reinforce the importance of their consistent performance and the value it brings to the project. Celebrate significant project milestones, and their efforts in mentoring and helping others.

# Five additional points to consider

Executives and senior managers would agree that everyone has a role to play in project leadership, as it aligns with the growing emphasis on collaborative, cross-functional teams and empowering employees to take ownership of their work.

However, they will also emphasise the following points:

- **Clarity in roles and responsibilities:** While everyone should contribute to project leadership, it is essential to maintain clear roles and responsibilities within the team. Executives and senior managers will want to ensure that team members understand their specific contributions to the project's success and how they can lead within their areas of expertise.

- **Balancing empowerment with accountability:** Encouraging team members to take on leadership roles can be highly beneficial for project outcomes and team dynamics. However, executives and senior managers will also emphasise the importance of holding individuals accountable for their actions and decisions, ensuring that empowerment does not lead to a lack of focus or direction.

- **Providing support and guidance:** For team members to effectively contribute to project leadership, they may require training, mentoring and coaching from more experienced leaders. Executives and senior managers can play a vital role in creating a supportive environment that fosters learning and development, enabling team members to grow as leaders.

- **Encouraging open communication and collaboration:** Executives and senior managers would stress the importance of fostering a culture of open communication and collaboration within the team. By creating an environment where team members feel comfortable sharing their ideas, concerns and feedback, they can actively participate in project leadership and contribute to the project's success.

- **Recognising and rewarding leadership:** To promote project leadership at all levels, executives and senior managers should recognise and reward team members who demonstrate effective leadership skills. This can help to reinforce the idea that leadership is not limited to formal positions but can be demonstrated by anyone on the team who contributes positively to the project's objectives.

In the next three chapters, you will discover the three pillars of project leadership:

- **Self leadership** – who I am
- **Solution leadership** – how I do it
- **Practice leadership** – what I do

Each pillar has five ingredients. It is the integration, effort and fine-tuning of team skills, people engagement and delivery approach that creates the real impact. So, with that in mind, let's get stuck in.

# PILLAR

# SELF LEADERSHIP

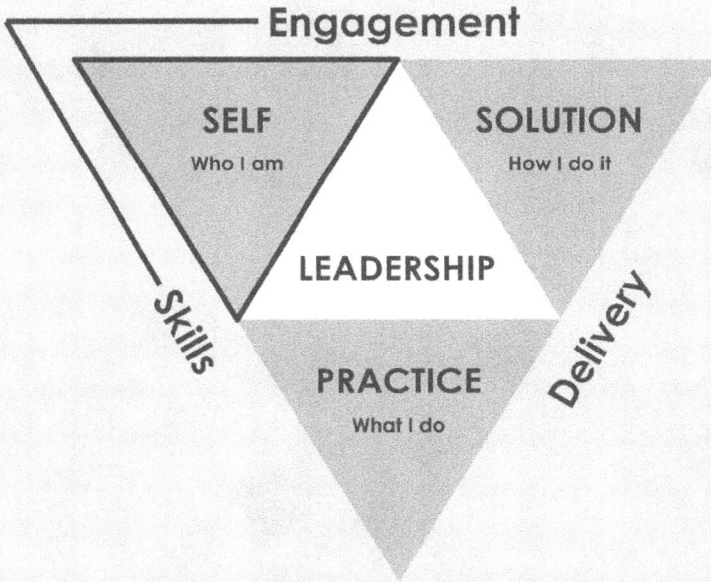

Engagement

SELF
Who I am

SOLUTION
How I do it

LEADERSHIP

Skills

PRACTICE
What I do

Delivery

**Self Leadership** is the ability of an individual to understand and manage themself to be more effective in leading others. It requires introspection and development in five key ingredients: **self-awareness**, **values and principles**, a **growth mindset**, **resilience**, and **self-discipline**. Self Leadership underscores the belief that before leading others, you must be capable of leading yourself.

# Self-awareness

Self-awareness is like looking in a mirror. But instead of seeing only your external appearance, you see the internal aspects of yourself – thoughts, feelings, motivations and beliefs. The mirror shows all the blemishes and imperfections, as well as the beauty and strengths, allowing you to truly understand yourself, just as you are.

Self-aware project teams understand how their feelings and behaviours affect the people around them, allowing them to manage their emotions and respond effectively to different situations.

How do you respond to feedback, setbacks or trying something new?

Do you get goosebumps or a tingling feeling when you hear someone share a story? Do you feel butterflies in your stomach when you are anxious or nervous? Do you feel angry or disappointed when someone lets you down?

These are all self-awareness triggers that spark an inner dialogue, and they matter. Triggers act as mirrors, reflecting aspects of your internal world that might remain unnoticed in everyday life.

They offer opportunities for growth by illuminating areas that might benefit from increased attention or development. They can facilitate better decision making, and improve interpersonal relationships by enhancing your understanding of personal motivators, emotional responses and behavioural patterns.

Does Emily's story resonate with you?

Emily, a project manager at a renowned tech agency, was known for her sharp intellect and impeccable work ethic. Her team often marvelled at how she juggled complex projects with apparent ease. However, beneath this facade of perfection, Emily grappled with challenges unseen by those around her.

Her life was a whirlwind of deadlines, meetings and an ever-growing list of responsibilities. On the surface, she was the epitome of success – a role model for her peers. But internally, Emily was in turmoil. She felt constantly overwhelmed, struggling to keep up with her own standards of perfection.

This internal struggle began to seep into various aspects of her life – work, relationships and well-being.

While she managed projects in a calm manner, decision making became increasingly stressful. Emily found herself second-guessing every choice, worried about the repercussions of each action. The once fulfilling job started to feel like a burden.

Her personal relationships began to fray as well. The little time she spent with friends and family was overshadowed by her preoccupation with work. Conversations were distracted, and her patience grew thin.

Emily's health took a back seat. Skipping meals and cutting down on sleep became common as she tried to find more hours in the day to work.

The turning point came with a crucial project – a project that Emily had spearheaded with enthusiasm. Due to her mounting stress and diminishing focus, she missed a critical flaw in the project plan. The oversight led to a significant delay and cost overrun.

This incident was a jolt to Emily. She was forced to confront the fact that her way of functioning was unsustainable. The realisation that her pursuit of perfection and lack of self-awareness were harming her work, her team and her personal life was a bitter pill to swallow.

As Emily sat quietly, reflecting on the recent events, she recognised that change was necessary. She understood that her first step was to look inward, to understand herself beyond the facade of the competent project manager. It was time to unravel the tangled web of her thoughts and feelings, to discover what truly mattered to her, and to align her life with these revelations.

'Self-awareness is being able to accept your weaknesses while focusing all of your attention on your strengths.'

– Gary Vaynerchuk (Gary Vee)

Consider a project team devoid of self-awareness. Miscommunications run rampant, conflicts brew, and the collaboration that's typical for project success remains elusive.

Now, envision a self-aware team. Every member, attuned to their strengths and weaknesses, navigates through the project, mitigating personal and collective hurdles with grace and strategic finesse. The latter scenario breathes life into project execution, doesn't it?

## How self-awareness elevates project teams

By understanding their own communication styles, and being mindful of their colleagues', team members foster a communication ecosystem that is clear, empathetic and effective. Self-awareness translates to recognising when a message isn't being conveyed or received effectively and adjusting the approach accordingly.

When individuals comprehend their emotional triggers and behavioural patterns, it paves the way for healthy conflict resolution and nurtures a positive working environment. Knowing 'the self' enables team members to approach conflicts with a solution-oriented mindset, ensuring disagreements pave the way for innovation rather than discord.

A self-aware team is akin to a well-oiled machine. Members, aware of their own and their teammates' strengths and weaknesses, ensure that tasks are allocated effectively, aligning skills with project needs. This not only elevates the quality of work but also ensures that every member is contributing in a manner that maximises their potential.

Self-awareness fosters resilience. Teams that are aware of their collective emotional and strategic landscapes adapt more effectively to challenges, navigating through project roadblocks with an adaptive and proactive approach.

# Developing self-awareness

The first step towards self-awareness is taking time to self-reflect. This involves pausing and paying attention to your thoughts, feelings and behaviours without judgement. Techniques such as mindfulness meditation can facilitate this by helping you stay present and fully engaged with your current state of being.

Seek constructive feedback from others and be open to it. Sometimes, we have blind spots that are only visible to others. Trusted friends and family, or even a professional like a counsellor or coach, can provide valuable insight into patterns or behaviours that you might overlook.

Writing down thoughts and feelings can help uncover patterns and recurring themes in behaviour, and increase your understanding of your emotions. It provides a space for introspection, allowing you to notice and reflect on subconscious patterns.

Learning to identify and manage your emotions can significantly boost self-awareness. This can be done by regularly assessing your emotional state and analysing your responses to certain situations. Understanding why you react in a certain way can give you deeper insight into your emotional makeup.

Understand what matters most to you. What are your core values? What are your goals? Aligning your actions with your values and goals can help you make decisions that feel authentic and right for you, thereby increasing your self-awareness.

Remember, self-awareness is a journey, not a destination. It's a continuous process of learning and growth that requires effort, dedication and honesty.

The ripple effects of self-awareness in project teams extend far beyond the immediate goals. It cultivates a culture of transparent communication, robust problem solving, and collective growth. Projects become not just tasks to be completed but also opportunities for individual and collective development.

# INGREDIENT #2

# Values and principles

What's important for you may not be important for me!

That statement, said to me by a senior executive, hit me in the face. I was presenting at a project board meeting, highlighting an item at risk that needed attention. I had never experienced such a blunt and dismissive response from this senior executive. I had to pause to understand what to say or do next. After the meeting, I approached her to try and understand if there was something I could do differently. She apologised and indicated she may have been in the room but her mind was elsewhere.

A 2021 *Harvard Business Review* article,[6] titled 'High-Performing Teams Start with a Culture of Shared Values', states:

> *'The link between values and performance isn't always immediately obvious. But consider that culture and values are how an enterprise honours its mission and it becomes clear that values are a crucial component of strategic intent. For example, throughout his tenure, Steve Jobs' commitment to fusing design with technology was*

*a value that attracted both customers and talent. More recently, Tim Cook has been leveraging the value of privacy in much the same way.'*

We enter a workplace with a suitcase packed with values, formed and polished by personal experiences, cultural contexts and social norms. These values, whether it's the emphasis on integrity, diligence, innovation or empathy, act as internal compasses, guiding decision making and behaviour. But in the busyness of project environments, these individual compasses often point in several varying directions.

For example, Sally, a seasoned marketer, might prioritise innovation, always searching for the next creative campaign. In contrast, John, the meticulous data analyst, may prioritise precision and caution. Here, diverse individual values are not a threat but an asset, forming a vibrant spectrum that can illuminate varied paths towards solutions and growth.

**'Your beliefs become your thoughts, your thoughts become your words, your words become your actions, your actions become your habits, your habits become your values, your values become your destiny.'**

– Mahatma Gandhi

Values and principles, whether for an individual or a project team, serve as foundational guides that influence behaviours, decisions and interactions. Let's explore what these might mean for you and your project team.

# Your personal values and principles

Your values are like your personal guiding light, illuminating the path you should take, especially when faced with dilemmas or decisions that challenge you ethically or morally.

When you encounter choices, your values and principles become a decision-making framework, helping you select options that align with what you believe is right and ethical.

Your daily actions, reactions and interactions are shaped by your values, ensuring consistency in how you relate with others and manage tasks.

Your values help in shaping your identity, allowing you to present yourself authentically to others, fostering genuine relationships.

# Your project team's values and principles

Values and principles act as a unifying force within a project team, ensuring that all members are aligned and moving towards common objectives.

They shape the culture of the project team, determining how members interact, communicate and solve problems together.

Clearly defined values and principles set the standard for expected behaviours and practices within the team, ensuring a healthy working environment.

In instances of conflict or disagreement, shared values and principles offer a blueprint for resolution in a way that is agreeable and fair to all team members.

Consistency in adhering to shared values enhances trust among team members, which is crucial for collaboration, communication and overall project success.

# Practical examples

Here are some hypothetical ways you can act out specific values and principles, individually and as a team.

## Value: Integrity

*For you:* This might mean always being honest in your communications and transparent about your work progress, even when things aren't going as planned.

*For the team:* This could translate to cultivating an environment where members feel safe to voice concerns, share ideas and admit to mistakes without fear of blame.

## Principle: Collaborative decision making

*For you:* You might prioritise seeking input from your peers before making decisions that impact the team.

*For the team:* This principle ensures that decisions made at the project level are inclusive, considerate of diverse perspectives, and are communicated transparently to all members.

Your personal values guide your internal compass, while shared team values and principles foster a cohesive and collaborative working environment. Balancing personal and team values is crucial for maintaining your integrity while contributing positively to the project team's dynamics and success.

INGREDIENT #3

# Growth mindset

The journey to a mountain peak is long and demanding, filled with obstacles and setbacks. A self-leader, like a mountaineer, understands that the climb is more than reaching the summit; it's about the lessons learned, the resilience built, and the skills acquired along the journey.

> **'Whether you think you can or think you can't, you're right.'**
>
> – Henry Ford

In every project, challenges are not just inevitable but necessary. Where a fixed mindset might perceive hurdles as daunting pitfalls, indicating their limited capabilities, a growth mindset frames them as opportunities. Every obstacle becomes a stepping stone, providing valuable lessons which, when analysed and understood, become catalysts for innovative solutions and strategies. Thus, a project team that welcomes challenges rather than shying away from them fosters a culture of problem solving and continuous improvement.

Carol S. Dweck, author of *Mindset: The New Psychology of Success*, found that employees in growth-mindset organisations are:

- 47% more likely to see their colleagues as trustworthy,

- 34% more likely to feel a strong sense of ownership and commitment to their companies,

- 65% more likely to say their companies support risk taking, and

- 49% more likely to say their companies foster innovation.

# The continuous carousel of a growth mindset

With a growth mindset, individuals perceive change not as a threat but as an opportunity to extend their skill set. Continuous learning becomes the norm, whereby each team member proactively seeks to expand their knowledge, be it through workshops, courses or knowledge-sharing sessions. This constant upskilling not only boosts individual proficiency but also elevates the collective competency of the team, ensuring the project remains agile and relevant in a rapidly evolving landscape.

Project timelines are often dotted with pitfalls and setbacks. The lens of a growth mindset shifts the perception of failure from a negative outcome to a vital, informative experience. Each setback becomes a lesson, offering insights that can streamline processes, refine strategies, and ultimately steer the project towards its goals. This positive spin on failure also nurtures a safe environment where team members feel empowered to take calculated risks, innovate, and explore new avenues without the paralysing fear of failure.

Constructive feedback, whether praise or criticism, is a powerful tool for personal and project growth. While a fixed mindset might perceive criticism as a threat or a validation of inadequacy, a growth mindset sees it as fuel for progress. It becomes a mirror, reflecting the areas that require attention and improvement. When team members openly give, receive and act on feedback, it not only accelerates individual growth but also propels the project forward by ensuring continuous refinement of strategies and processes.

A project team stitched together with a growth mindset fosters a culture that is resilient, adaptable and innovative. It assures that each member, while navigating through their individual paths of growth, is simultaneously contributing to an environment that is conducive for collective learning and progress.

Nurturing a growth mindset in a project team ensures a framework where challenges are opportunities, continuous learning is paramount, failure is a stepping stone, and feedback is a mechanism for refinement. It crafts a setting where individual and collective growth harmoniously propel the project towards success, ensuring that every milestone, whether a triumph or a lesson, contributes meaningfully to the journey towards the ultimate objective.

# Be mindful of barriers and bridges

Remember, having a growth mindset is not about being perfect or immediately excelling. It's about believing in the potential for development, being open to new experiences, persevering through challenges, and seeing every interaction as a chance to learn and improve.

Several factors can prevent a project team member from developing or maintaining a growth mindset:

- Fear of making mistakes or failing can hinder them from trying new things or stepping out of their comfort zone. They may stick to familiar tasks and avoid challenges, which limits their learning and growth opportunities.

- Having a team culture that does not promote learning, development and adaptability could manifest as a lack of mentorship, lack of opportunities for professional development or a culture that punishes mistakes.

- Without the right support and guidance, they may feel lost and overwhelmed, which can discourage them from taking risks. They may not know where to begin or how to tackle new challenges.

- When they are exhausted or stressed, they are less likely to pursue learning opportunities, take on challenges, or feel optimistic about their potential for growth.

- Feedback is crucial. If team members are not receiving regular, constructive feedback, they may not know what areas they need to improve upon or how to do so.

Overcoming these barriers often requires a combination of individual mindset shifts, supportive project practices, and an organisation that values learning and growth. Here are some suggestions:

- Instead of avoiding or feeling threatened by challenges, view them as opportunities to learn and grow. When faced with a difficult task, frame it as a puzzle to solve or a chance to expand your skills. Remember, it's okay not to have all the answers immediately; it's about the journey of finding them.

- Instead of shying away from feedback or taking it personally, actively seek it from peers, supervisors and other stakeholders. Constructive feedback can provide insights into areas of improvement, and even positive feedback can highlight areas to further strengthen. Approach feedback with the question 'How can this help me improve?', rather than defending or justifying actions.

- While achieving goals and results is important, it's equally essential to celebrate the effort and hard work that goes into the process. Recognise and reward perseverance, resilience and dedication in yourself and in peers. This shift in perspective will ensure a consistent drive to not fear failure.

- Always look for opportunities to learn and grow. This can be through formal training, workshops, reading or even learning from peers. Embrace the idea that there's always something new to learn, and that your existing skills and knowledge can always be enhanced. This continuous learning cycle ensures adaptability and relevance in a rapidly changing project environment.

- Instead of viewing setbacks or mistakes as failures, see them as valuable feedback. Analyse what went wrong, identify the lessons learned, and determine how to approach similar situations differently in the future. By shifting the narrative from 'I failed' to 'I learned', team members can maintain motivation and drive even in the face of obstacles.

By consistently practising these actions, a project team member not only fosters a personal growth mindset but also contributes to creating a culture of growth and continuous improvement within the team. This, in turn, can lead to more innovative solutions, better collaboration and, ultimately, more successful project outcomes.

INGREDIENT #4

# Resilience

The first thing that comes to mind when I hear the term 'resilience' is the words *'knocked down, get up again'*.

According to Dr Karen Blay from Loughborough University, *'resilience in projects is defined as; the capability of a project to respond to, prepare for and reduce the impact of disruption caused by the drifting environment and project complexity. The dimensions of resilience are; proactivity, coping ability, flexibility and persistence.'*[7]

Every project will have setbacks. What is important is how you respond – let's look at an individual response and a team response.

## Individual resilience versus team resilience

Lucy is known for her individual resilience. Over her illustrious career, she has weathered numerous storms. When a project she was leading for a major client was faced with unexpected regulatory changes, many thought it would collapse. But Lucy stood firm. With her agile mindset, she quickly adapted her plans to align with the new regulations, put in extra hours, and managed to deliver the project successfully on time. Lucy's resilience was her strength. She could single-handedly steer projects through the roughest waters.

Bob, on the other hand, led his projects with a focus on team resilience. When one of his key projects hit a major obstacle – a critical system failure that resulted in a massive data loss – the project seemed destined for failure. Unlike Lucy, Bob didn't shoulder this challenge alone. Instead, he called for an urgent team meeting.

In the meeting, he encouraged his team to openly share their feelings about the setback. Bob emphasised the importance of treating this failure as a shared responsibility and an opportunity for collective growth. The team members brainstormed together, with Bob carefully fostering an environment of mutual trust and respect. One of the junior developers suggested a recovery method he had learned at a recent tech conference. They collectively decided to give it a try and, to their relief, it worked. The data was recovered and, with combined efforts, the team managed to deliver the project successfully.

Both types of resilience are crucial in a project setting. Project managers like Lucy showcase the importance of leading from the front, while project managers like Bob demonstrate the power of collective effort and resilience in navigating adversity. To build truly resilient organisations, you need to foster both individual and team resilience, combining the unique strengths of both approaches.

# Building individual resilience

Building personal resilience is not just beneficial for the individual; it also significantly contributes to the overall resilience of the project team. Here are some ways to help you build personal resilience, thereby enhancing the team's resilience:

- **Practice self-awareness:** Understand your emotional responses and triggers. Self-awareness allows you to manage your reactions and maintain composure during stressful situations, setting a positive example for the team.

- **Maintain a positive attitude:** A positive outlook can be infectious and can significantly boost team morale. Focus on finding solutions rather than dwelling on problems, and express optimism about the team's ability to overcome challenges.

- **Strengthen stress management skills:** Develop strategies for managing stress, such as mindfulness, meditation, exercise, or engaging in hobbies. Managing personal stress effectively prevents it from spilling over into the team environment.

- **Prioritise self-care:** Ensure you are looking after your physical and mental health. A healthy team member is more productive and can contribute more effectively to the team's objectives.

- **Seek feedback and continuous learning:** Be open to feedback and committed to continuous learning and self-improvement. This not only enhances your skills but also contributes to the team's collective knowledge and capability.

- **Build a support network:** Cultivate relationships both within and outside the team. A strong support network can provide advice, perspective, and a sounding board for ideas and challenges.

When individual team members are resilient, they are better equipped to handle pressure, adapt to change and bounce back from setbacks.

# Building team resilience

You want project teams who can effectively navigate challenges, learn from setbacks, and continue moving towards their objectives despite adversities. Here are some ways to help you do that:

- Encourage project team members to see challenges and setbacks as opportunities to learn and grow. This mindset can promote a culture of continuous improvement and innovation.

- Create an environment where project team members feel comfortable sharing their ideas, concerns and failures. This can foster trust and collaboration, and enable more effective problem solving.

- Promote flexibility and adaptability in the face of change. This can help the project team to navigate more effectively unexpected shifts in project scope or timelines.

- Ensure that project team members have access to the resources and support they need to successfully navigate challenges. This could include providing training in resilience-building techniques, access to mentoring or coaching, or other forms of support.

- Regularly acknowledge and celebrate project team successes, no matter how small. This can help to boost morale and motivation, and reinforce a positive, resilient mindset.

- After a setback or challenge, facilitate a project team discussion to reflect on what happened, what was learned, and how this learning can be applied in the future. This can help to turn setbacks into opportunities for growth and development.

Building these attributes into your team's way of working will enhance its resilience and improve its ability to succeed in an ever-changing project environment.

# INGREDIENT #5

# Self-discipline

Cambridge Dictionary defines self-discipline as '*the ability to make yourself do things when you should, even if you do not want to do them.*'[8]

> 'Discipline is the bridge between
> goals and accomplishment.'
> – Jim Rohn

Imagine a neatly arranged domino set-up. A single flick and each piece meticulously topples the next, embodying a chain of systematic events. Now envisage each domino as a team member. The stability, direction and certainty of each piece (or person) are encapsulated in self-discipline.

When each member diligently performs their roles, abstaining from procrastination and distraction, the project flows seamlessly, resembling the domino effect, whereby tasks are executed, and milestones are achieved coherently — all in a timely manner.

# Infusing discipline into team DNA

Incorporating self-discipline within a team requires a steady, consistent effort from each member, gradually blending into a work rhythm. The work of a disciplined project team not only results in successful project delivery but also cultivates a healthy, productive and positive work environment.

Individual team members must harbour a sense of personal accountability. This involves acknowledging one's roles and responsibilities and executing them with honesty. Small steps, like setting personal deadlines and adhering to them, can foster a disciplined approach towards task completion.

Pre-planning equips the team with a clear pathway. Ensure that every task, right from minor to major, is planned, including contingency buffers for unforeseen delays.

A discipline in communication is paramount. Decide upon fixed times for team check-ins and updates. Utilise communication tools that facilitate organised conversations and file sharing, ensuring that all members are across project progress.

Respecting time is a formidable aspect of self-discipline. This involves starting meetings promptly and respecting the working hours of team members. A disciplined respect of each other's time and efforts fosters a positive working environment.

Recognise and applaud the disciplined efforts of team members. This not only bolsters their morale but also sets a precedent for the importance of self-discipline within the team.

Now let's talk three key tactics — plan, share, check. While each team member practises self-discipline, it's vital to stitch these efforts into a collective pattern. Here's how:

- **Joint planning sessions:** Involving all members in planning sessions ensures that each person is aligned with the project's objectives and understands their role in achieving them.

- **Opportunities to openly share:** Creating spaces for open conversations, where team members can express challenges they might be facing in maintaining discipline, can lead to collaborative solutions and shared understanding.

- **Periodic check-ins:** Weekly or bi-weekly check-ins, where each member updates the team on their progress, not only keeps the project on track but also cultivates a disciplined approach towards regular reporting and task execution.

Embrace, empower, and let the dominoes of disciplined efforts cascade towards successful project completions.

# Six tips for self-discipline

If you want to incorporate self-discipline within a team, you need to lead by example. Here are six simple ways to do that:

- **Consistency in actions:** Work towards your goal, even when it's tough or you don't feel like it.

- **Time blocking:** Prioritise three things and set aside time to work on them regardless of your mood or external circumstances.

- **Self-control:** Say 'no' to immediate gratification in favour of long-term success.

- **Perseverance:** When facing obstacles or setbacks, bounce back and try again.

- **Routine and habits:** Prioritise regular movement, nourishing meals and adequate sleep.

- **Responsibility:** Accept responsibility for actions and don't blame others when things go wrong. Take steps to correct mistakes or improve situations, instead of waiting for others to do it.

# Self Leadership Reflection

Remember, the five ingredients of self leadership are: **self-awareness, values and principles, a growth mindset, resilience,** and **self-discipline**.

Here are five questions I encourage you to reflect on. Think of a project or situation you have experienced and note the behaviours and actions back then. Now after reading about self leadership how would you approach a similar project or situation next time.

1.  How would you describe your level of self-awareness? Can you identify instances where your actions were influenced by your emotions?

2.  What are your core values and principles? How do they influence your leadership style?

3.  Do you have a growth mindset or a fixed mindset?

4.  How do you react to failures and setbacks? Are you resilient in the face of adversity?

5.  How disciplined are you in achieving your goals? Can you provide examples of when you had to exert self-discipline to meet a project deadline?

# Self Leadership Checklist

Use this checklist to track over time how you have developed your self leadership strengths. Tick what you are consistently doing well and select three you are going to focus on next.

- o   I am aware of my strengths and weaknesses.
- o   I manage my emotions effectively.
- o   I see failures and challenges as opportunities for learning.
- o   My actions align with my core values and principles.
- o   I display confidence in my decisions and actions.
- o   I practise self-discipline to meet project objectives.
- o   I actively seek out opportunities for personal growth and development.
- o   I am comfortable with ambiguity and uncertainty.
- o   I can align my personal values and goals with my work.
- o   I exhibit high emotional intelligence in my interactions with others.

- o  I practise self-care and promote a healthy work-life balance.
- o  I am capable of self-motivation and do not rely on external validation.
- o  I reflect regularly on my behaviour and its impact on others.
- o  I am self-aware and understand my strengths and weaknesses.
- o  I am proactive and do not need to be prompted to take action.
- o  I continuously learn and adapt based on my experiences.
- o  I am resilient and can handle stress effectively.
- o  I am motivated and persistent in achieving my goals.
- o  I take responsibility for my actions and decisions.
- o  I can manage my time and priorities effectively.

# PILLAR

2

# SOLUTION LEADERSHIP

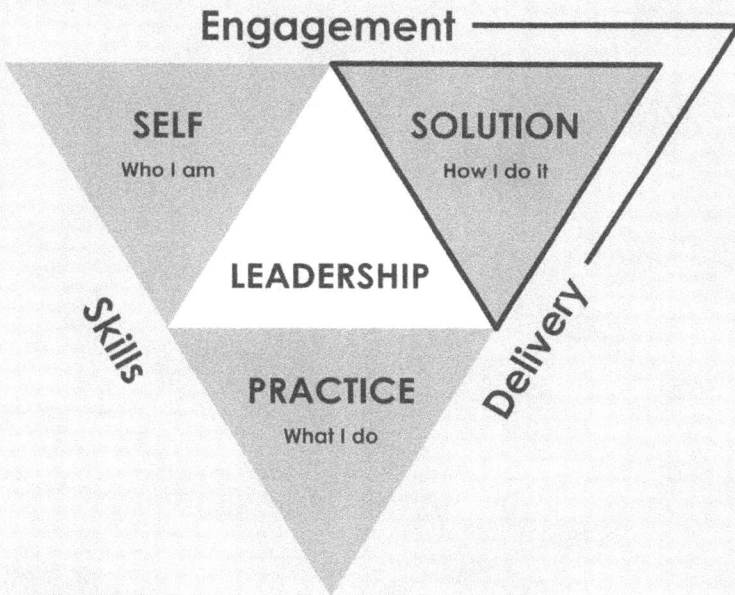

Engagement

SELF
Who I am

SOLUTION
How I do it

LEADERSHIP

Skills

PRACTICE
What I do

Delivery

**Solution Leadership** revolves around the ability to navigate through challenges and uncertainties to deliver viable solutions. This involves five key ingredients: **critical thinking** to analyse situations, **innovation** to design novel approaches, **adaptability** to pivot as needed, **problem-solving** to address issues, and **risk management** to mitigate potential setbacks.

# INGREDIENT #6

# Critical thinking

According to a survey conducted by the World Economic Forum, employers consider critical thinking one of the top ten skills needed for jobs in 2025.[9]

Critical thinking is like the judicial process in a court. Just as a judge or jury would gather and scrutinise evidence, listen to different perspectives and carefully consider all the facts before reaching a verdict, a critical thinker weighs up all the available information, considers varying viewpoints and reaches a reasoned conclusion based on their analysis.

Successful projects, from technology implementations to marketing campaigns, hinge on critical thinking, the ability to think clearly and rationally, understanding the logical connection between ideas. It's about elevating a project team's approach to solving problems, making decisions, and learning new concepts.

This means stepping back from immediate issues or tasks, examining them with a discerning eye, questioning initial perceptions and finding optimal solutions based on evidence and reason.

# Project X

Let's step through Project X, responsible for creating a new online educational platform that could accommodate a vast number of students and offer a wide range of subjects. The platform was intended to be user-friendly and capable of providing personalised learning paths for each student.

After months of development, the beta version of the platform was ready, and the team started pilot testing it with a small group of users. However, initial feedback was disappointing. Users reported that the platform was confusing to navigate and lacked the personalised experience they expected.

Instead of getting disheartened or hastily making surface-level adjustments to the platform, the team decided to apply critical thinking to solve the problem. They collected and analysed the feedback in detail, looking for patterns and recurring issues. They also looked at how users interacted with the platform, using heat maps and user recording tools to understand where users were struggling.

One critical insight came from a junior developer, Sarah, who pointed out that the team had assumed they understood what 'user friendly' and 'personalised learning' meant without asking their user base. Sarah proposed conducting a series of user interviews and surveys to gather more in-depth qualitative data.

The project team was initially hesitant about conducting comprehensive user research that would take time and resources, but recognised the value in Sarah's suggestion.

They decided to pause the development and invest in this critical research phase. The team surveyed and interviewed students, teachers and e-learning experts, asking targeted questions to understand their needs and preferences better.

The findings from the research were eye opening. Users wanted a simpler, more intuitive interface and more flexibility in customising their learning paths, with recommended courses based on their interests and learning styles.

With these insights, the team revamped the platform. They simplified the navigation, developed an algorithm for personalised course recommendations, and provided users with more control over their learning paths. When the updated platform was retested with the user group, the feedback was overwhelmingly positive.

Thanks to critical thinking, the team behind Project X didn't simply react to initial negative feedback. Instead, they dug deeper to understand the root cause of the issue. They questioned their assumptions, gathered more data, analysed it thoroughly, and used those insights to revise their approach. As a result, they successfully developed an educational platform that truly met their users' needs.

'We cannot solve our problems with the same thinking we used when we created them.'

– Albert Einstein

# Six ways to encourage critical thinking

By harnessing the power of critical thinking, you'll be able to watch your project teams transform challenges into opportunities, and objectives into achievements. Here are six ways to do it:

## Curious minds

Imagine a team where curiosity isn't just welcomed; it's celebrated. Recognise and applaud those team members who dare to dig deeper, who look beyond the obvious, and who aren't afraid to ask 'why' or 'what if'. When you honour these curious minds, you're not just encouraging a person; you're fostering a culture of exploration and innovation.

## Constructive debates

Think of your team discussions as brainstorming arenas, where diverse ideas clash, dance, and merge to create something extraordinary. Encourage constructive debates, where every voice is heard and every perspective valued. In these vibrant exchanges, ideas are not just shared; they are sculpted, stretched and strengthened.

## Analytical approach

Equip your team with an analytical mindset, turning them into detectives unravelling the mysteries of each challenge. Approach problems not as roadblocks but as puzzles waiting to be solved. This mindset opens up pathways to innovative solutions that may have remained hidden under conventional thinking.

## Power of the question

In a world where answers are often prized more than questions, dare to be different. Cultivate an environment where questioning is the norm, not the exception. Encourage your team to delve into the depths of every problem, every project, every assumption. Remember, the quality of our questions often dictates the quality of our answers.

## Pivot with purpose

The business world is ever-changing, and rigidity can be the Achilles heel of any project. Teach your team the art of agile thinking – to assess the impact of their decisions continuously and pivot when necessary. This agility allows your team to adapt and thrive in the face of new challenges and changing landscapes.

## The goldmine

Regard every project, every task as a learning opportunity. Implement findings from retrospectives into future actions. This isn't just about learning from mistakes; it's about building on successes and constantly evolving. By turning reflections into actionable insights, you ensure that every project leaves a legacy of knowledge and growth.

# INGREDIENT #7

# Innovation

What comes to mind when you think of innovation? The latest gadget? Innovation extends beyond things you will find in a catalogue. It is the ability to conceive, develop, deliver and scale new products, services, processes and business models for customers.

> 'The heart and soul of the company
> is creativity and innovation.'
>
> – Bob Iger, CEO of The Walt Disney Company

## An innovation hub

Emma's mornings typically began with a stroll to her local coffee shop. Today, she noticed something different. Instead of the familiar menu, a sign stood proudly proclaiming, 'Our Coffee, Your Imagination'.

With curiosity piqued, she approached the counter. Raj, the ever-cheerful barista, was bubbling with excitement. He explained their new concept: not just serving coffee but co-creating experiences. He spoke of a wish box where customers could suggest what they desired in a coffee experience.

Emma, always full of ideas, mentioned her longing for a quiet corner in cafes. She loved writing but found the ambient noise too distracting for brainstorming sessions. Almost in response, Raj gestured to a new addition to the cafe: a silent pod with a whiteboard, aptly named the 'Brainstorm Brew Booth'.

Raj's next suggestion was even more intriguing. The cafe was now crafting drinks inspired by stories. The theme of a customer's novel, a poem or even a personal anecdote could become the essence of a beverage.

Caught up in the innovative spirit, Emma shared the premise of her novel, a sun-drenched romance with an undercurrent of mystery. Taking this theme to heart, Raj brewed a unique concoction for her: a cold brew infused with floral notes, crowned with a hint of spice, embodying summer love and intrigue.

As Emma settled into the silent pod, sipping her personalised brew, she marvelled at how her local cafe had transformed from just another coffee shop into a hub of inspiration, demonstrating that the essence of innovation lay in recognising and fulfilling unspoken needs.

## Five ways to unleash innovation

Amid the ever-present challenges of tight deadlines, resource constraints and ambitious goals, the role of innovation might often seem secondary. But it's this very ingredient that can elevate a team from achieving deliverables to unlocking exceptional results. With that in mind, here are five ways to unleash innovation in your project team:

## Cultivate an environment welcoming all ideas

- **Open idea channels:** Establish regular forums or meetings where team members can freely present ideas. These can be formal sessions like 'Innovation Hours' or informal set-ups like a digital idea board.

- **No idea too small:** Reinforce the notion that no idea is too trivial or too ambitious. Sometimes, a small tweak suggested by a team member can lead to significant improvements in a process or product.

- **Recognition and reward:** Acknowledge and celebrate ideas that are brought to the table, even if they aren't implemented. This encourages a culture of continuous idea sharing.

## Fostering a mindset that embraces failure

- **Reframe the narrative:** Communicate that each failed attempt is a stepping stone to success. Share stories of well-known innovations that were born out of repeated failures.

- **Learning reviews:** Instead of traditional post-mortem meetings that focus on what went wrong, conduct learning reviews to understand what can be learned from failed attempts.

- **Risk-taking budget:** Allocate a certain percentage of the project budget for experimentation, acknowledging that some of these funds might not lead to direct success but are crucial for learning.

## Encouraging diverse perspectives

- **Diverse teams:** Build teams with members from varied backgrounds, experiences and skill sets. This diversity fuels a broader range of ideas and solutions.

- **Cross-functional collaboration:** Regularly rotate team members across different roles or pair them with members from other departments for short-term collaborations.

- **Cultural sensitivity training:** Conduct workshops that emphasise the value of different perspectives, helping team members understand and appreciate the richness that diversity brings.

## Adapting to the emerging landscape

- **Agile methodologies:** Implement agile practices that allow for flexibility and rapid response to change, rather than sticking rigidly to initial plans.

- **Stay informed:** Regularly update the team on industry trends, emerging technologies and market dynamics. This keeps everyone attuned to the changing environment.

- **Scenario planning:** Engage in regular scenario planning exercises to anticipate possible future changes and brainstorm how the team would adapt to these scenarios.

## Leveraging technology as an active participant

- **Tech-enabled solutions:** Integrate technology solutions that can automate routine tasks, thereby freeing up time for team members to focus on more innovative work.

- **Data-driven decision making:** Utilise data analytics tools to gather insights that can drive innovative strategies and decisions.

- **Tech exploration time:** Allow team members dedicated time to explore and experiment with new technologies, software, or tools that could potentially be beneficial for the project.

Remember, innovation isn't just about grand ideas but also the small, consistent steps towards doing things better, smarter and more efficiently. Every challenge faced, every task tackled, should carry the footprint of innovation, leading the path to not just success but also transformative results.

# INGREDIENT #8

# Adaptability

Research by the McKinsey Global Institute suggests that by 2030, approximately 375 million workers globally will need to make significant changes to their skill sets due to automation and artificial intelligence, underscoring the need for adaptability in the workforce.[10]

About fifteen years ago, I was participating in a strategy think tank when someone said, 'We need to unlearn'... This was followed by silence and many, including me, were left scratching their heads. What does that have to do with change and solutions?

'The illiterate of the 21st century will not be those who cannot read and write, but those who cannot learn, unlearn, and relearn.'

– Alvin Toffler in his book *Future Shock* (1970)

# Learn, unlearn, relearn

Now let's imagine a grand, wooden bookshelf filled with books of all sizes and colours, representing the vast knowledge and experiences accumulated over a lifetime.

**Learn:** Every new book added to the shelf represents the acquisition of fresh knowledge, a novel skill, or a new experience. Just as a reader eagerly dives into a new book's pages, excited by its unique story and lessons, learning allows you to continuously enrich your personal library with diverse and updated content.

**Unlearn:** Over time, some books become outdated, irrelevant, or take up valuable space that could be occupied by more relevant information. Removing a book from the shelf to make room for new ones mirrors the process of unlearning. It's about recognising that holding on to outdated beliefs or redundant information can stifle growth. By letting go, you free up space, ensuring your bookshelf remains organised and functional.

**Relearn:** Now, imagine taking an old favourite from the shelf, dusting it off, and discovering it has been updated with new chapters or revised content. This represents relearning. It's not about discarding the old entirely, but revisiting and refreshing your understanding with a modern perspective. Like a classic novel with a new foreword or additional content, relearning enhances your existing knowledge, making it more relevant to the current context.

The bookshelf encapsulates the dynamic journey of continuous growth, where you consistently add new insights, let go of what's no longer serving you, and refresh your perspectives to stay relevant and informed. For project teams, this means embracing adaptability to ensure they not only survive but thrive in the good and bad days of project planning and delivery.

# Applying the formula to project teams

The secret formula for adaptability is simple: learn, unlearn, relearn. In this section, I explain why each element is so important in project teams, and how to apply it.

## Learn: Embrace continuous learning

The journey begins with the fundamental principle of continuous learning. It means consistently seeking out new knowledge, tools, methods and practices that can enhance the team's efficiency and effectiveness.

*Why it matters:* As projects evolve, teams often confront unexpected challenges or opportunities. Having a culture of continuous learning equips the team with an ever-expanding toolkit to address these twists and turns, ensuring the team remains agile and responsive.

How to embrace:

- Beyond standard training sessions, implement structured learning programs with clear objectives and outcomes – like a learning lab or allocating block time for reading articles.

- Ensure learning is not a separate activity but integrated into daily work through practical application – like shadowing and observing to understand a day in the life of others.

- Encourage a collaborative learning environment where team members learn from each other's experiences and expertise – like regular personal showcases.

## Unlearn: Let go of the outdated

Perhaps the most challenging element, yet the most crucial, is the act of unlearning. It involves discarding practices, beliefs or methods that no longer serve the team's purpose. It's about acknowledging that just because something worked in the past doesn't mean it's the best approach for the future.

**Why it matters:** Holding on to outdated practices can hinder innovation and efficiency. For a project team to be truly adaptable, it must be willing to shed the old to make way for the new.

How to improve:

- Create dedicated sessions where the team reflects on current practices and openly discusses what might need to be discarded or altered – like think tanks or what if sessions.

- Foster an environment where team members feel safe to question the status quo without fear of criticism – remember to practise listening and no judgement.

- Discard your own outdated practices and encourage others to follow suit – demonstrate and share the benefits.

# Relearn: Update and upgrade

Learning doesn't end once a particular method or tool has been adopted. As the external environment shifts – be it due to technological advancements, changes in stakeholder requirements, or shifts in market dynamics – previously learned skills or methods might need updating.

**Why it matters:** A strategy or tool that was effective a year ago might be obsolete today. Project teams must be attuned to these changes, ensuring that their approaches remain current and relevant.

How to enhance:

- Implement feedback loops that allow the team to regularly assess and adjust their methods based on the latest data and feedback.

- Utilise mentorship and coaching to guide team members, offering them support and insight – like an adopt a buddy program.

- Use adaptive learning strategies that cater to individual learning styles and speeds, ensuring everyone keeps pace with the changes.

When project teams embrace the mantra of 'learn, unlearn, relearn', they're positioning themselves for success. This is because it allows them to:

- Pivot quickly in response to unexpected challenges, ensuring project timelines and goals remain on track.

- Foster a culture that values continuous learning, is unafraid to discard the outdated, and naturally promotes innovation.

- Consistently update tools and methods, and work within teams operating at peak efficiency, ensuring resources are utilised optimally.

- Better respond to changing stakeholder needs, ensuring the product or solution aligns with requirements and expectations.

In a constantly changing world, adaptability is no longer just a 'nice to have'. It's essential and about organisations remaining future-ready.

INGREDIENT #9

# Problem solving

There are several warning signs that a project team is facing challenges that need their attention:

- Not communicating effectively, missing meetings and misunderstandings.

- Consistently missing deadlines.

- Decreasing motivation and increased frustration.

- New features, tasks or requirements keep getting added without proper assessment.

Although it may be obvious there are issues, I am sure there are project teams who ignore these signs, hoping the problem will go away. In contrast, effective project teams not only identify problems but also analyse their root causes and actively work towards implementing solutions.

## The 'five whys' problem-solving technique

Originating from the Toyota Production System and developed by Sakichi Toyoda, a Japanese inventor and industrialist, the 'five whys' is a problem-solving technique that seeks to identify the root cause of issues by asking 'Why?' repeatedly, usually five times, until the fundamental cause is unearthed. The main objective of the method is to move beyond superficial symptoms and diagnose the underlying problem, ensuring long-term resolution rather than temporary fixes.

When a problem is identified, the question 'Why did this happen?' is posed. The answer forms the basis for the next 'Why?' question. This process is repeated until a root cause is identified, which typically occurs by the fifth 'Why?', although the actual number can vary.

The 'five whys' method promotes deep thinking, encourages a systematic approach to problem solving, and can often unveil solutions that are both simple and cost-effective. Here's an example, showing a specific problem and the root cause of that problem, which was identified as a result of asking five 'Why?' questions:

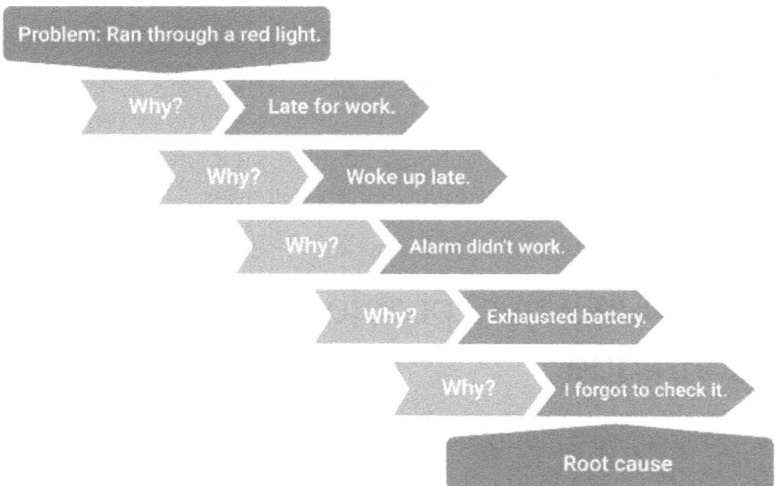

Imagine if a project team looking at this problem jumped to a technical solution to fix or replace the alarm rather than updating a process work instruction. This would result in time and cost wastage, and likely the problem would reappear at some stage.

# Four tips to ensure problem-solving success

Is your project team tackling the right problem and addressing the correct 'Why?' response? Here are some tips to ensure problem-solving success:

## Form a team

- Assembling a cross-functional team is crucial for comprehensive problem solving. Different team members bring unique insights based on their expertise, experiences and delivery perspectives. This diversity can lead to more innovative and effective solutions.

- *Tip:* When forming a team, consider including members from various functions such as architecture, design, marketing, finance and operations. This approach ensures that all aspects of the problem are examined, and solutions are viable across the organisation.

## Define the problem

- Clearly defining the problem is akin to setting the stage for effective problem solving. A well-articulated problem statement helps in maintaining focus and prevents the team from veering off course.

- *Tip:* To create a clear problem statement, describe what is happening, where it's happening, its effects on the project, and why it matters. Ensure that this statement is specific, measurable, and agreed upon by all team members.

## Ask why

- Facilitating the 'five whys' process helps delve into the underlying cause of the problem. This technique, grounded in factual data rather than emotional responses, leads to a deeper understanding of the issue.

- *Tip:* When a "Why?" question leads to multiple responses, consider each as a separate branch for investigation. This approach helps in identifying multiple root causes and addressing them comprehensively. Ensure that the facilitator is skilled in guiding discussions, keeping them focused and objective.

## Take action

- Identifying the root cause is only half the battle; the next crucial step is implementing a solution. Solutions can be categorised into strategic changes, which might require additional resources and funding, and operational changes, which are part of the ongoing process improvement.

- *Tip:* For strategic changes, prepare a detailed business case highlighting the benefits, required resources, and potential ROI to secure necessary approvals and funding. For operational changes, integrate the solution into existing processes, ensuring continuous monitoring and adjustment as needed.

## Further considerations for problem-solving success:

- **Documentation and communication:** Throughout the problem-solving process, maintain detailed documentation and ensure clear communication among all team members and stakeholders. This transparency helps in keeping everyone aligned and informed.

- **Follow-up and feedback:** After implementing a solution, it's important to follow up to assess its effectiveness. Collect feedback from the team and stakeholders to understand the impact of the solution and make adjustments if necessary.

- **Learning and adaptation:** Encourage a culture where every problem and its resolution is viewed as a learning opportunity. Adapt and refine problem-solving strategies based on past experiences and lessons learned.

Problem solving in project teams is not an isolated event but an ongoing, iterative process. It necessitates a blend of analytical thinking, creativity, collaborative effort and strategic execution to navigate through the complex challenges that projects invariably present. By embedding a robust problem-solving framework, project teams can enhance their resilience, agility and success rate, crafting a path that meticulously negotiates around obstacles and leads towards project completion and success.

# Risk management

Are you a risk taker or risk averse? You probably answered, 'It depends!' The 'depends' is based on the reward or what you are willing to pay for something to happen.

> ### 'Risk is the price you pay for opportunity.'
> – Tom Selleck

Imagine a ship sailing through a stormy sea. The captain and the crew must constantly assess the potential risks – the strength of the wind, the height of the waves, and the ship's ability to withstand these conditions. Similarly, a project team is like a ship navigating through potential risks – timeline delays, resource shortages, or unexpected technical hurdles.

## Risk takers versus the risk averse

Individuals often steer their ships influenced by their perception of, and outlook towards, risk. Risk takers and risk-averse individuals sail with significantly different compasses, each embarking on journeys that distinctly shape their decisions, experiences and outcomes.

Risk takers are often envisaged as the daring sailors:

- They accept uncertainty as part and parcel of the journey, and are generally undeterred by the lack of a clear path.

- They are more likely to explore new opportunities, trying out different approaches or solutions that have not been validated.

- They tend to make decisions swiftly, guided by intuition, opportunity and potential, sometimes overlooking exhaustive analysis.

- They are resilient and adapt quickly to failures, viewing them as learning opportunities and stepping stones to eventual success.

In contrast, those who are risk averse sail with caution:

- They prioritise stability and predictability, often opting for routes that are well mapped, even if it means slower journeys and smaller rewards.

- They typically avoid ventures where the outcome is uncertain and instead opt for strategies that minimise their exposure to potential losses.

- They tend to delve into detailed analysis before making decisions, weighing pros and cons meticulously.

It's crucial to recognise that risk taking and risk aversion are not absolute.

Optimal risk decision making and action often involves a balance – a kind of calculated risk taking where the potential downsides are acknowledged and mitigated to the extent possible, and opportunities are not bypassed merely due to the presence of risk. This balanced approach – often referred to as risk management – enables project teams to navigate through both calm and stormy seas, ensuring sustainability and progression.

# Finding the right balance of risk

Understanding the risk orientation of the project team – in shaping strategies, making decisions and leading towards successful delivery – ensures they embrace opportunity and are not anchored by fear and anxiety. Here are some ways to help you strike the right balance of risk in your project team:

## Assessing the team's risk orientation

- **Evidence-based approach:** Observe and gather evidence on the team's past decision-making patterns – risk registers and stakeholder feedback. Are there instances where they have taken calculated risks that paid off? Or are there situations where excessive caution may have led to missed opportunities?

- **Feedback mechanisms:** Implement regular feedback sessions or retrospectives to understand the team's comfort level with risk. This can help in identifying whether the team leans more towards risk taking or risk aversion.

## Cultivating an open risk discussion environment

- **Encouraging open dialogue:** Create forums or regular meetings where team members feel safe to voice concerns, speculate about potential risks, and propose mitigation strategies.

- **No-blame culture:** Foster a culture where mistakes or misjudgements in risk taking are not met with blame but are seen as learning opportunities.

## Inclusive risk identification and mitigation planning

- **Diverse Perspectives:** Involve team members from different functions and levels of the project to bring in a variety of viewpoints. This diversity can lead to more robust risk identification and innovative mitigation strategies.

- **Stakeholder Engagement:** Ensure that stakeholders are not just informed but also actively involved in risk discussions. Their insights, especially from those who have a high stake in the project's success, can be invaluable.

## Recognition and celebration of effective risk management

- **Acknowledging success:** Recognise and celebrate instances where effective risk management led to project milestones being met or crises being averted. This can be done through formal acknowledgements in team meetings, newsletters, or even informal team gatherings.

- **Storytelling:** Share stories of successful risk management within the team and the wider organisation to inspire and educate others.

## Encouragement and reward for innovation in risk management

- **Rewarding innovation:** Establish rewards or recognition programs for team members who come up with innovative risk management solutions or improvements.

- **Continuous learning:** Promote a culture of continuous improvement where the team is encouraged to refine their risk management practices based on past experiences and learnings.

Ultimately, finding the right balance of risk in project management is about creating a dynamic where the team is neither paralysed by fear of failure nor recklessly chasing high-risk opportunities. It's about instilling a sense of confidence and competence in handling risk in a way that aligns with the project's goals and the organisation's overall strategy.

# Solution Leadership Reflection

Remember, the five ingredients of solution leadership are: **critical thinking, innovation, adaptability, problem solving,** *and* **risk management**.

Here are five questions I encourage you to reflect on. Think of a project or situation you have experienced and note the behaviours and actions back then. Now after reading about solution leadership how would you approach a similar project or situation next time.

1.  How often do you use critical thinking in your role?

2.  How do you foster innovation within your team?

3.  How adaptable are you to changing situations?

4.  How do you approach problem solving?

5.  How do you manage risks in your projects?

# Solution Leadership Checklist

Use this checklist to track over time how you have developed your solution leadership strengths. Tick what you are consistently doing well and select three you are going to focus on next.

- o I use logical and creative approaches to solve problems.

- o I analyse information from different perspectives before making decisions.

- o I encourage creativity and experimentation within my team.

- o I identify potential risks early and develop plans to mitigate them.

- o I can effectively analyse and make use of feedback.

- o I am able to see the bigger picture beyond the immediate problem.

- o I foster a culture of innovation and creativity within my team.

- o I am capable of translating complex ideas into understandable and actionable items.

- o I am able to clearly define problems before seeking solutions.

- o I am comfortable taking calculated risks when necessary.

- o I take into account the long-term impact and potential unintended consequences of solutions.

- o I can modify or pivot solutions based on changing circumstances or new information.

- o I am skilled at prioritising issues and focusing on the most impactful problems.

- o I ensure my team has the resources and knowledge necessary to solve problems.

# PILLAR

# PRACTICE LEADERSHIP

**Engagement**

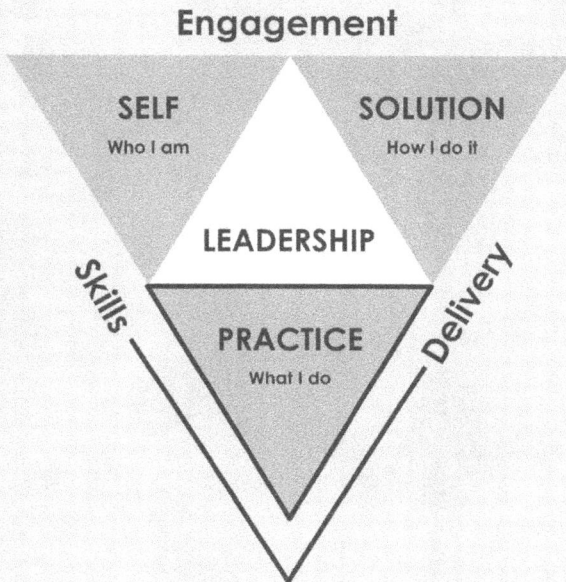

SELF
Who I am

SOLUTION
How I do it

LEADERSHIP

Skills

Delivery

PRACTICE
What I do

**Practice Leadership** is about translating strategy into execution by employing a set of practical leadership ingredients such as effective **decision making, building and leading teams,** clear and impactful **communication,** skilful **delegation** and astute **performance management.** This pillar is crucial in ensuring that theoretical strategies and plans are pragmatically implemented and produce desired outcomes.

# Decision making

Do you have a decision log? If you do, how does the team go about implementing a decision?

'A real decision is measured by the fact that you've taken new action. If there's no action, you haven't truly decided.'

– Tony Robbins

## Three types of decisions faced by project teams

Project teams are faced with three types of decisions – strategic, tactical and progress. Each type of decision has its own level of importance and impact, and understanding the differences can help project teams prioritise and address challenges effectively.

According to the Project Management Institute's 2018 Pulse of the Profession report, 9.9% of every dollar spent by organisations is wasted due to poor project performance, which is often the result of poor decision making.[11] Meanwhile, a McKinsey report suggests that improving the decision-making process can result in 20% better decision outcomes and a 15% reduction in meeting times.[12]

With those statistics in mind, here's an overview of strategic, tactical and progress decisions.

## Strategic decisions

These decisions are typically long term, made infrequently, often occur at project establishment or at major milestones, require significant analysis, and involve executive management or project sponsors. Examples include:

- Deciding on the main project objectives and allocating budget items.
- Choosing the primary technology stack or platform for a software development project.
- Evaluating and selecting primary vendors or partners for the project.

## Tactical decisions

These decisions translate the high-level objectives into actionable plans, usually occur at the beginning of project stages or releases, need to adapt to evolving requirements, and involve the project sponsor, project manager and key stakeholders. Examples include:

- Determining the suitable delivery methodology and frequency of status meetings.

- Recruitment of team leads and team members.

- Setting short-term goals and milestone markers.

## Progress decisions

These are quick decisions made daily or even multiple times a day as challenges arise and circumstances change to keep the project on track. They're usually made by individuals or small teams who are directly involved in the project issue. Examples include:

- Resolving a minor conflict between team members.

- Adjusting a team member's task for the day based on emerging priorities.

- Choosing to escalate an issue to higher management.

- Deciding on a workaround for a minor technical glitch.

# Good and bad decisions

Decision making is like being at a crossroads. You need to choose which way to go based on the information you have about each path. You evaluate the available options based on your knowledge and choose the one that seems most likely to get you to your destination or project goal.

Whether it is a strategic, tactical, or progress decision, project teams and stakeholders consider them as either good or bad without fully understanding the decision-making process.

**Context:** The quality of a decision is often heavily context dependent. What makes a decision good or bad isn't just the decision itself, but how it aligns with the current circumstances, goals and available information. A decision that seems optimal in one context might be poor in another.

**Dynamic:** Decisions are made based on the information and resources available at the time. A strategic decision that seems sound today might turn out to be less effective as market conditions, company dynamics, or external environments change.

**Evaluate:** A decision is typically deemed good if it leads to successful results and aligns with the intended goals. Conversely, it might be considered bad if it leads to undesirable outcomes. However, it's crucial to note that some decisions, especially good ones, may not deliver immediate positive results, and its true value can only be judged in the long term.

**Learn:** Sometimes a decision considered bad due to negative outcomes can provide valuable lessons and insights, leading to better decisions in the future. Similarly, a good decision that produces positive results can reinforce effective strategies and approaches.

**Risk:** Especially in strategic and tactical decisions, there are always elements of uncertainty and risk, which means even well-thought-out decisions have the potential to turn out poorly. The key is in risk assessment and management.

**Judgement:** Different stakeholders may have varying opinions based on their perspectives, interests, and the aspects of the outcome they prioritise.

Here's an example of progress decision making done well...

At a tech start-up, Sophie and her team were responsible for developing a new mobile app. During testing, one afternoon, Sophie noticed a minor glitch where the app would hang for a couple of seconds after a specific user action. The glitch wasn't listed as a known issue, and the official launch was just a week away.

Instead of brushing it off as a minor concern or waiting for someone else to notice, Sophie quickly convened a small meeting with her immediate teammates. Together, they reproduced the glitch, confirmed its source, and brainstormed solutions. One of Sophie's colleagues suggested a minor code adjustment that might fix the problem without causing disruptions elsewhere.

Sophie, taking the lead, decided to implement this quick fix. After rigorous testing, they found that the issue was resolved without introducing any new problems. They documented the change and informed their supervisor of the proactive measure. The app was launched successfully, and the team was commended for their attention to detail and rapid response.

And here's an example of progress decision making gone wrong...

David worked at a marketing firm, overseeing a team responsible for sending out weekly email newsletters to subscribers. One morning, David was informed that the link to the main article in the newsletter was broken, a few hours before the scheduled send-out.

Instead of addressing the issue immediately, David assumed it would be a quick fix and decided to work on another project. When he returned to the email issue an hour later, he realised it wasn't as simple as he thought. The problem stemmed from a miscommunication with the content team, and the article wasn't even ready to be published.

With time running out, David made a hasty decision to replace the main article link with another to a less relevant article without consulting his team. The newsletter went out, but the company received numerous complaints from confused subscribers who were expecting the originally promoted content.

David's delay in addressing the problem, combined with a hasty decision, resulted in a hit to the company's reputation among its subscribers. The incident served as a lesson in the importance of timely responses and proper communication.

Both stories highlight the significance of progress decisions in day-to-day project environments. A proactive, team-centric approach can lead to success, while delays and lack of communication can lead to preventable errors and challenges.

# Seven steps for effective decision making

Effective decision making often involves a structured process to ensure that all relevant information is considered, and that the best possible decision is reached given the circumstances. Here are seven steps you can take:

- **Identify the decision:** Clearly define the nature of the decision you must make. Understanding the decision's significance and context is crucial at this stage.

- **Gather information:** Collect all relevant information for making the decision. This might involve researching, asking others for input, or simply reflecting on personal experiences that might inform the decision.

- **Identify the options:** Based on the information gathered, generate a list of possible options. There's usually more than one path to a desired outcome.

- **Weigh the evidence:** Evaluate the pros and cons of each option. This can involve prioritising what's most important, anticipating potential outcomes, or considering others' advice. Tools like a decision matrix can be helpful at this stage.[13]

| SIMPLE DECISION MATRIX | | | |
|---|---|---|---|
| | OPTIONS | | |
| Criteria | Car A | Car B | Car C |
| Cost | 5 | 3 | 3 |
| Practicality | 2 | 4 | 3 |
| Performance | 4 | 2 | 5 |
| Reliability | 1 | 2 | 4 |
| Fuel Economy | 2 | 3 | 3 |
| TOTAL | 14 | 14 | 18 |

- **Choose the option:** After considering all the options, choose the one that seems to be best suited to the situation.

- **Take action:** Act on your decision. Implement the choice that has been made.

- **Review the decision:** After implementing the decision, reflect on the outcome. Did things go as expected? What worked and what didn't? This final step is crucial for learning and improving decision-making skills for the future.

This process can be used for both simple and complex decisions, although the amount of time and effort spent on each step may vary accordingly. Remember, it's okay to revisit previous steps if you realise new information should be taken into account.

INGREDIENT #12

# Team building

Walking into a new project team on day one can indeed be a kaleidoscope of sensations and perceptions, often swinging between two extremes.

Imagine entering a workspace for the first time and being engulfed in an almost tangible aura of discomfort. The atmosphere is thick with unspoken tension, like a dense fog that muffles and distorts. You can almost hear the silent hum of unease. Every corner of the room seems to echo with an unsettling quietude, broken intermittently by hushed voices that seem to carry an undercurrent of urgency or dissatisfaction. The desks, cluttered with papers and personal items, appear as isolated islands of activity in a sea of disconnection. Whiteboards, stark and unutilised, stand as silent witnesses to the lack of collaboration or shared vision. There's an omnipresent sense of busyness, a superficial flurry of activity that somehow, paradoxically, hints at a stagnancy in real progress. The most notable movement is the collective, almost synchronised departure at day's end – a clear sign of relief, an escape rather than the conclusion of a fulfilling day's work.

Contrast this with stepping into a different project team environment where the vibe instantly warms and welcomes you. The air buzzes with a low, harmonious hum of activity — a sound that speaks not just of work being done, but of connections being made. There's a rhythm to the interactions; conversations flow seamlessly from serious discussions to light-hearted banter, painting a picture of mutual respect and easy camaraderie. Desks are lively with activity, yet there's an underlying order and purpose to their arrangement. Whiteboards burst with colourful notes and diagrams — vivid testaments to collective brainstorming, planning and achievement. The energy in this space is different; it's vibrant and dynamic, yet comforting and inclusive. Walking into this team, even as a newcomer, feels like finding a missing piece of your professional puzzle. You sense an almost immediate belonging, an unspoken assurance that here, in this team, you're not just another cog in the machine but a valued member of a thriving, collaborative community.

A project team vibe — or project team culture — can be an indicator for project success or project failure.

A project team vibe, distinctly different from overarching organisational culture, encapsulates the unique microcosm of attitudes, interactions and emotional climate within a specific team. It's the palpable energy that buzzes through the team's daily interactions and shapes their collective ethos. This vibe is not so much defined by written policies or formal procedures as it is woven from the interpersonal dynamics, communication styles, shared experiences, and even the unspoken understandings that team members develop over time.

# The benefits of team building

## 'Alone we can do so little; together we can do so much.'

### – Helen Keller

The vibrancy and depth of a project team's vibe is not an instant phenomenon. It's a rich tapestry woven over time, evolving through shared experiences, consistent effort, and the gradual melding of individual personalities into a cohesive unit.

On day one, or when a new member joins, the atmosphere of a project team is often more tentative and exploratory. Initially, it might sound like conversations filled with formalities and cautious exchanges, as members are still gauging one another's communication styles, boundaries and professional temperaments. The environment is more akin to a polite meet-and-greet: people are still discovering common ground and shared interests, and the air is tinged with a sense of expectancy and uncertainty.

Building the kind of team dynamic where ideas flow freely and camaraderie blends seamlessly with professionalism requires time. It necessitates a series of ice-breaking sessions, consistent team-building exercises, open and empathetic communication, and, importantly, shared challenges and successes. Each member's integration into the team is a journey, characterised by gradually lowered guards and deepening trust.

As the team navigates through various project phases and confronts both setbacks and achievements, they learn to lean on each other. The collective response to these experiences shapes the team's identity. The members learn, adapt and grow together, moving from cautious formal interactions to a more open and spontaneous exchange. This transformation doesn't happen overnight; it's fostered by the team's active participation and willingness to engage not just at a professional level but on a more personal, human level as well.

Thus, it's important to acknowledge and facilitate this gradual evolution. Recognising and celebrating small milestones in team cohesion and interpersonal understanding can encourage this growth, helping to build a team that is as focused on its members' well-being as it is on achieving project success.

Team building is crucial for project team success for several reasons:

- **Fosters better communication:** Team-building activities can help to break down barriers and improve communication between team members. Better communication leads to improved understanding and cooperation, which helps to enhance overall team performance.

- **Promotes collaboration:** Team building encourages team members to work together more effectively. It helps to break down silos and promotes a culture of collaboration and mutual support.

- **Enhances problem-solving skills:** When team-building activities involve problem-solving tasks, team members can enhance their capacity to strategise and brainstorm. This can be beneficial when facing complex project tasks.

- **Boosts team morale:** Team building can help to make work more enjoyable and meaningful. This can lead to increased job satisfaction, improved morale and higher productivity.

- **Identifies and utilises strengths:** Team-building activities can help to identify the strengths of individual team members. These strengths can then be better utilised within the team, leading to more effective team performance.

- **Improves team cohesion:** Team building helps to create a sense of unity and common purpose. This can improve the team's ability to work together effectively and achieve project objectives.

A project team, reassured by the trust, understanding and communication nurtured through team-building endeavours, can navigate through challenges with a shared resilience and a collective solution-oriented mindset. The strategic synergy, cultivated through well-designed team-building activities, not only strengthens the internal dynamics but also enhances the external delivery of the team, ensuring projects are executed with optimal efficiency, creativity and quality.

# The blueprint of effective team building

A 2020 Gallup article, titled 'Lead Your Remote Team Away from Burnout, Not Toward It', states, *'Loneliness is emotional. Isolation is structural. And your remote employees are likely experiencing both. What's dangerous is that one study found workplace isolation can derail productivity up to 21%.'*[14] Additionally, according to teambuilding.com, Australia is currently ranked third in the list of countries investing in virtual team building, behind Singapore and the United States.[15] As remote work and virtual teams become increasingly common, how can you ensure effective team building? Here's an eight-step blueprint:

- **Identify the objective:** Start by identifying what you hope to achieve from the team building. The objective could be anything from improving communication to fostering innovation.

- **Plan activities aligned with the objective:** Plan activities that are in line with your objectives. These could be problem-solving tasks, team sports or creative projects, among other things. Ensure the activities are engaging and inclusive.

- **Set clear guidelines:** Make sure everyone understands the guidelines for each activity. This will help to ensure that everyone can participate effectively.

- **Foster a supportive environment:** Encourage everyone to participate, and ensure the environment is supportive and non-judgemental. This will help to promote openness and honesty.

- **Facilitate the activities:** The role of the facilitator is crucial in team building. They need to guide the activities and ensure everyone has a chance to participate.

- **Debrief after each activity:** Discuss the activities afterwards. This can help to reinforce the lessons learned and apply them to the project team's work.

- **Apply lessons to work:** Take what was learned during the team-building exercises and apply it to the work environment. This will help to ensure that the benefits of the team building are carried over into the project.

- **Review and repeat:** Regularly review the benefits of the team-building activities, and repeat them as necessary to reinforce the learning and keep the team spirit alive.

Remember, team building is not a one-off activity. It's an ongoing process that should be part of the project team's culture. The most successful teams regularly engage in team building to continually improve their performance and effectiveness.

# Other team-building ideas you can try

A formal strategy or blueprint is not the only way to foster team building. Here are some additional team-building tactics you and your team can experiment with:

- **Fun activities:** Engage in activities that require collaboration. This could be anything from escape room challenges and scavenger hunts to trivia nights and team sports.

- **Coffee break chats:** Encourage team members to take coffee breaks together.

- **Potluck lunches or themed food days:** Host a potluck lunch where everyone brings a dish to share, or a themed food day like Taco Tuesday or Pizza Friday.

- **Recognition boards:** Set up a board where team members can acknowledge each other's achievements and hard work.

- **Think tanks:** Have regular brainstorming sessions where every idea is welcomed and valued. Make it fun by setting a theme, using visual aids, and offering prizes for the most creative or innovative ideas.

- **Learning circles:** Organise learning circles where team members can share their skills or knowledge about a topic they are passionate about. It could be anything from process tips to drawing lessons.

- **Icebreakers at meetings:** Start meetings with an engaging question (icebreaker) that allows team members to share something about their personal lives or interests.

- **Fitness challenges:** Encourage a healthy lifestyle with group fitness challenges. This could be a step count challenge, a weekly group yoga session, or a virtual fitness challenge for remote teams.

- **Celebration of personal milestones:** Celebrate team members' birthdays, work anniversaries or personal achievements.

INGREDIENT #13

# Communication

Have you ever been in a meeting or observed a conversation and noticed conflict, chaos or confusion? Of course you have, and no doubt you have been a participant in that frustrating and difficult situation on more than one occasion. Let's face it – we all have relationships we need to work at, particularly our communication.

Good communication is like a traffic control system in a bustling city. It manages the flow of information, ensures everyone is heading in the right direction, and prevents 'accidents' or misunderstandings from causing project gridlocks.

## Profound insights into the dynamics of communication

Let me take you to a picturesque country town, where a project team including key stakeholders gathered for a planning workshop to kick off a large project. The morning was filled with presentations and brainstorming sessions, but the post-lunch hours were reserved for fun and team-building games.

One of the chosen activities was 'Pass the Message', more commonly known as 'Chinese Whispers'. The game involves participants sitting in a line or a circle. The first person whispers a message into the ear of the next person in line, who then passes it on in a whisper to the next person, and so on. The final person says the message out loud, and it's often amusing to see how much the message has changed from the original.

Molly, the HR manager, started the game by whispering a sentence to Jake, seated to her right. The original message was: 'ME Solutions will launch a new virtual reality project next month.' As the message travelled down the line of twenty workshop participants, whispers turned into hushed giggles, puzzled looks and raised eyebrows. By the time it reached Lisa, the last person in line, everyone was eager to hear the transformed message.

With a confident smile, Lisa stood up and announced, 'ME Solutions' new vacation is a reality next quarter!'

The room erupted in laughter. Some hoped that the transformed message meant an additional holiday next month. The playful distortion of the message brought a light-hearted moment to the workshop. The game, while entertaining, offered profound insights into the dynamics of communication:

- **Information degradation:** Just like in the game, in real-world scenarios, messages often get distorted when passed through multiple intermediaries. It emphasises the importance of direct communication, especially for critical information.

- **Assumptions:** At various points in the whispering chain, individuals might fill in gaps or make assumptions based on partial information, leading to a deviation from the original message.

- **Importance of feedback:** The game highlights the significance of feedback loops. If participants in the middle could have checked back with Molly about the accuracy of the message, the final version might have been closer to the original.

- **Listening skills:** Active listening is essential. In the game, any lapse in concentration can alter the message, much like in professional settings where not paying full attention can lead to misunderstandings.

- **Clarity is key:** Ensuring that messages are clear and easily understandable can prevent unnecessary confusion.

At the end of the game, the team not only shared a good laugh but also took away some valuable lessons about communication, making the workshop both fun and insightful.

# Effective communication with stakeholders

Project teams talk about and develop effective communication plans, yet I am not convinced they spend the time implementing and reviewing them.

'The most important thing in communication is hearing what isn't said.'

– Peter Drucker

Project teams should consider these elements for effective communication with their stakeholders (who will have varying needs and demands for information to make decisions and accept the changes going on around them):

**Repetition:** Emphasising a point by repeating it several times can enhance understanding and retention.

**Responsibility:** If the message is still not being understood after several repetitions, it suggests the communicator must re-evaluate their approach.

**Clarity:** Ensure that the message is clear, concise and free of jargon.

**Channel:** Utilise various communication channels to disseminate the message effectively.

**Engagement:** Make sure the message is engaging and relevant to the audience.

**Templates:** Use templates for consistency in curating and presenting content.

**Feedback:** Seek feedback to understand if the message is being understood as intended.

**Adjustment:** Be willing to modify the communication style, content or channel based on feedback and observed outcomes.

# Effective communication among team members

The following activities, when thoughtfully implemented and consistently practised, can significantly enhance the communication capabilities of a project team, leading to improved collaboration, reduced misunderstandings and, ultimately, more successful project outcomes.

## Establish clear communication protocols

- **Channels:** Define and utilise specific channels for various kinds of communication (for example, Slack for informal and email for formal).
- **Templates:** Use templates for standard communications to ensure consistency.

## Offer regular updates and check-ins

- **Daily stand-ups:** Implement brief daily meetings to discuss completed tasks, upcoming work and potential obstacles.
- **Weekly reviews:** Host weekly sessions to discuss progress, review timelines and adjust plans as necessary.

## Maintain transparency and openness

- ***Open-door policy:*** Encourage team members to share ideas, concerns and feedback openly.

- **Shared documentation:** Use collaborative tools like Google Workspace or Microsoft Teams for transparent documentation and progress tracking.

## Create defined roles and responsibilities

- **RACI matrix:** Use a RACI (responsible, accountable, consulted and informed) matrix to clearly define each team member's role.

- **Onboarding:** Ensure that every team member is familiar with their duties and expectations.

## Embrace active listening

- **Listening workshops:** Conduct workshops to enhance active listening skills among team members.

- **Feedback sessions:** Establish mechanisms for giving and receiving constructive feedback.

## Facilitate inclusive communication

- **Diverse communication styles:** Acknowledge and adapt to the various communication preferences within the team.

- **Accessibility:** Ensure communication methods are accessible to all team members, considering any disabilities or remote-working challenges.

# Train and develop communication skills

- **Training sessions:** Invest in training programs focused on enhancing communication skills.

- **Mock sessions:** Engage in role play or mock sessions to practise crisis communication or client interactions.

# Utilise visual aids

- **Visual communication:** Use diagrams, charts and graphs to make complex data more digestible.

- **Prototyping:** Utilise prototypes or demos to provide a tangible understanding of concepts.

# Collaborate and co-create

- **Brainstorming sessions:** Encourage the collective development of ideas through regular brainstorming.

- **Collaboration tools:** Leverage tools like Miro or Asana to facilitate collaborative planning and idea sharing.

# Ensure cross-functional communication

- **Inter-team meetings:** Facilitate interactions between different teams to ensure alignment of objectives.

- **Cross-training:** Engage in sessions where teams can learn about the roles and challenges of their colleagues in different departments.

## Encourage informal communication

- **Social interactions:** Facilitate spaces for informal discussions and social bonding.
- **Team-building activities:** Engage in activities that foster team spirit and camaraderie.

## Provide periodic reviews and retrospectives

- **Project post-mortems:** Conduct reviews post-project to evaluate what went well and what didn't.
- **Continuous improvement:** Implement lessons learned from retrospectives in future projects.

## Celebrate and acknowledge

- **Acknowledgment:** Recognise and celebrate milestones, achievements and exceptional contributions.
- **Rewards and recognition:** Implement a system to reward team members who demonstrate outstanding communication or collaboration.

# INGREDIENT #14

# Delegation

While the essence of delegation – entrusting responsibilities and authority to others – remains the same, the particulars of how delegation is enacted within project teams can be shaped by the unique challenges, structures and demands of the project environment. Balancing the right mix of skills, navigating through tight timelines, and maintaining clear communication are key to effective delegation in a project context.

When you delegate tasks, it's like handing over the keys to your car. You're entrusting someone else to drive and you're expecting them to follow the right directions, obey the traffic rules, and reach the destination safely. You're still the car owner, but you're not in the driver's seat.

When diving into the workings of project delivery, delegation emerges as a pivotal concept built on authority, responsibility and accountability.

Authority represents the decision-making power and the ability to act that's granted to a team member. It's the trust placed in them to carry out a task, backed by the support and resources they need.

Responsibility encapsulates the duties and tasks that a delegate must effectively fulfil. It spells out what needs to be done, how it fits into the broader project, and the expectations tied to that role.

Accountability is the assurance that team members will stand by their work outcomes. Regardless of the results – be they triumphant successes or lessons learned from challenges – they remain committed to their role and its impact on the project.

# The importance of delegation in project teams

Within the dynamic environment of project teams, delegation stands out for the many benefits it brings to the table.

Efficiency takes the forefront. Delegation ensures that tasks are assigned appropriately within the team. Instead of one person being swamped with every detail, they can entrust certain tasks to others, streamlining the workflow and ensuring that every task gets the attention it merits.

Then there's development. Delegation is more than just offloading tasks; it's about investing in team members – providing opportunities for skill enhancement, experience acquisition and professional growth. It boosts morale and offers team members a chance to showcase and expand their abilities.

Productivity stands as another cornerstone benefit. A well-delegated team is like a well-oiled machine, where each member operates at their best capacity. When tasks align with individual expertise and capability, the project progresses more efficiently, achieving objectives more seamlessly.

In project management, effective delegation proves its worth time and again. It ensures that tasks find their best-fit executor, that team members are empowered and developed, and that the overall project workflow is optimised for success.

# Effective versus ineffective delegation

Lisa, who was handling a project to create a cutting-edge cybersecurity software, knew that the key to managing her multifaceted team was effective delegation. She took time to understand the unique skills and aspirations of each member, aligning their roles accordingly. Her main priorities were:

- **Skilful alignment:** Lisa assigned coding to Ethan, who had a knack for innovative problem solving, and placed Maria in charge of user experience, leveraging her eye for design and user-friendly functionality.

- **Empowering and trusting:** Lisa empowered her team by trusting them with critical decision making within their realms. She believed in their expertise and encouraged them to take ownership of their segments.

- **Regular check-ins:** However, she didn't leave them stranded. Regular check-ins, constructive feedback and an open-door policy ensured that each member felt supported and valued.

Lisa's project unfolded smoothly. Issues were promptly addressed, timelines were met, and the team felt a robust sense of accomplishment and unity. The final product was not only secure and efficient but also user-centric, ticking all the boxes for a successful project.

Meanwhile, Tom, managing a project on cloud storage solutions, took a drastically different approach. An adept coder and a meticulous planner, Tom had always found solace in handling things himself. This meant:

- **Holding the reins too tight:** Instead of dispersing tasks, Tom held on to them, believing it was quicker than explaining and overseeing. The design, coding and testing phases all bore his imprints, leaving little room for his team to contribute.

- **Disengagement and frustration:** The team, relegated to minor roles, felt underutilised and disengaged. Their skills rusted, and innovation dwindled as Tom became the singular driving force.

- **Burnout and delays:** Ultimately, Tom burnt out. Tasks slipped through the cracks, deadlines whooshed by, and the product, although functional, lacked the innovative spark it desperately needed.

Tom's project, while successful in developing a stable product, faltered in timelines and failed to harness the collective brilliance of his team. His team members, feeling uninvolved and unchallenged, were left seeking richer experiences and opportunities for contribution.

Both projects came to fruition but took divergent paths. Lisa's approach illustrated that understanding, empowering and effectively delegating to team members not only streamlines processes but also brews innovation and boosts morale. In contrast, Tom's journey underscored the perils of hoarding tasks: stunted team growth, lack of innovation and eventual burnout.

> 'We accomplish all that we do through delegation – either to time or to people.'
>
> – Stephen R. Covey

Consequences of ineffective delegation include:

- **Misalignment of skills and tasks:** If delegation isn't done thoughtfully, tasks might end up assigned to team members who lack the necessary skills or knowledge, leading to poor performance.

- **Loss of control:** Some project managers may feel they are losing control over the project when they delegate tasks. It's important to strike a balance between delegation and oversight.

- **Overburdening team members:** If not managed carefully, delegation can lead to some team members being overloaded with tasks, leading to stress and burnout.

- **Miscommunication:** If expectations aren't clearly communicated during the delegation process, it can lead to confusion, mistakes and inefficiencies.

- **Potential for shifting blame:** There can be a risk of accountability getting diluted or blame being shifted when tasks and responsibilities are not clearly defined and tracked.

# Eight steps of effective delegation

Delegation requires clear communication, trust and follow-through. It's a vital skill for project teams to master, to reap the benefits while mitigating the potential risks. There are eight steps to consider:

- **Identify tasks to delegate:** The first step is to determine which tasks can be delegated. Not every task is suitable for delegation. Tasks that are routine, require specific skills that team members possess, or are time-consuming but not necessarily critical for you to perform are good candidates for delegation.

- **Choose the right person:** This involves matching the task with the skills, abilities and capacity of the team members. It's important to consider the strengths and weaknesses of each team member, their workload and their professional development aspirations.

- **Clearly define the task and expectations:** When assigning a task, be clear about what the task involves, what the end product should look like and when it needs to be completed. Provide clear, concise instructions and ensure the team member understands them.

- **Provide necessary resources and authority:** The team member should be given the resources and authority to complete the task. This might include access to specific tools, a particular budget, or the authority to make certain decisions.

- **Establish a communication plan:** Set up regular check-ins to discuss progress, answer questions and provide guidance. However, avoid micromanagement. The aim is to provide support and direction, not to control every step.

- **Monitor progress and provide feedback:** Keep an eye on progress without interfering too much. Provide constructive feedback, both positive and negative, to guide the team member and help them improve.

- **Evaluate and learn:** After the task is completed, review the results. Did the outcome meet the expectations? What went well? What could be improved? This is a chance to learn and improve the delegation process for the future.

- **Acknowledge and reward:** Recognition is crucial in reinforcing positive behaviour and boosting morale. When a task is successfully completed, acknowledge the efforts and skills of the team member who was responsible.

Incorporating these steps into your delegation process will foster trust among team members, encourage skill development, and ensure the team is working effectively and efficiently.

INGREDIENT #15

# Performance management

For project teams, both performance management and feedback are essential. While feedback offers immediate insights, corrections and encouragement, performance management provides a structured approach to ensure the consistent and successful execution of a project. Understanding the distinction and value of each term ensures that they are used effectively and purposefully in the project environment.

Performance management is like a pilot flying an aircraft. The pilot sets the flight path (project goals), constantly monitors the systems and instruments (progress), communicates with the control tower (provides feedback), and adjusts the route based on weather conditions or air traffic (changes in the project scope).

Effective performance management is a continuous process, not a one-time event. It balances the benefits with potential drawbacks by being fair, transparent, collaborative, and focused on development of behaviours and processes rather than just measurement.

# Benefits and drawbacks of performance management

Here are some of the benefits of performance management:

- **Clarity and focus:** Clear performance expectations and targets help team members understand what's expected of them, allowing them to focus on their tasks and contribute more effectively to the project.

- **Improved productivity:** Regular monitoring and feedback can boost productivity. It helps to identify issues early and make necessary adjustments to stay on track.

- **Enhanced employee morale:** Recognition and rewards for good performance can increase morale and motivation. It promotes a positive work environment, which can further lead to higher productivity.

- **Better decision making:** Performance data collected through performance management aids in better decision making regarding resource allocation, team structuring and project direction.

- **Risk mitigation:** Ongoing performance management can help detect potential risks or issues early, allowing for proactive action to mitigate these risks.

- **Learning and development:** The feedback process can help employees understand their strengths and areas for improvement, providing them with opportunities for growth and development.

And here are some of the possible drawbacks of performance management:

- **Time and resource intensive:** Performance management can be time-consuming and may require significant resources, especially in large teams or complex projects.

- **Negative impact on morale:** If not handled correctly, performance management can lead to stress and reduce morale, particularly if the process is perceived as punitive rather than constructive.

- **Bias and inconsistency:** Performance management can sometimes be influenced by manager bias, leading to inconsistency and unfair appraisals. This can negatively affect employee trust and motivation.

- **Resistance to change:** Team members may resist changes in their performance expectations or feedback, particularly if they feel they're not involved in the goal-setting process or if changes are implemented without clear communication.

- **Overemphasis on metrics:** There's a risk of focusing too much on measurable performance and ignoring other vital aspects, such as creativity, innovation and teamwork.

# Ten steps to effective performance management

To ensure effective performance management of your project team, here are ten steps you can take:

- **Set clear objectives:** Each member of the project team should understand their specific role, what they are responsible for, and what the desired outcome of their work is. These objectives should be SMART: specific, measurable, achievable, relevant and time-bound.

- **Establish performance standards:** Develop measurable indicators or benchmarks to assess performance. These should be related directly to the project's objectives and each team member's role.

- **Prioritise effective communication:** Encourage open and honest communication. This includes clearly communicating expectations, providing consistent feedback and addressing any issues or concerns promptly.

- **Maintain regular monitoring and evaluation:** Consistently monitor the team's performance against the set standards. Regular check-ins or progress meetings can help keep everyone on track and address any issues promptly before they become significant problems.

- **Provide constructive feedback:** Timely, constructive feedback is crucial for performance improvement. Highlight what has been done well, as well as areas for improvement, and provide guidance on how to improve.

- **Offer training and development:** Identify gaps in skills or knowledge and provide opportunities for training and development. This helps improve the team's capability to meet their performance objectives.

- **Motivate and recognise:** Celebrate achievements and recognise good performance. This can be done through verbal recognition, rewards or other forms of appreciation. This not only motivates team members but also fosters a positive work environment.

- **Adapt and adjust:** Be prepared to revisit and adjust goals, strategies or processes as necessary. Flexibility is essential in project management as things may not always go as planned.

- **Conduct performance appraisals:** Conduct formal performance reviews at the end of significant project milestones or at the end of the project. This is an opportunity to assess overall performance, provide feedback and discuss plans for future projects or roles.

- **Strive for continuous improvement:** Use the lessons learned from each project to improve the performance management process. Continually refining your approach will lead to better project outcomes, and a more engaged and productive team.

Remember, performance management is a collaborative process. Including team members in the setting of objectives, standards and evaluations can help increase their engagement and ownership of the process.

# Tips for providing and receiving feedback

Regardless of whether you love or loathe feedback, it's an integral part of effective project management.

### 'Feedback is the breakfast of champions.'

– Ken Blanchard in his book
*The One Minute Manager* (1982)

So, with that in mind, here are some tips for providing feedback:

- **Be specific:** Rather than giving vague comments, point out specific instances or examples. Instead of saying, 'Your work was good', say, 'Your analysis on the market trends was thorough and added value to the presentation.'

- **Be constructive:** Feedback should provide direction for improvement. If you're pointing out an issue, offer suggestions on how it can be addressed.

- **Keep it relevant:** Stick to feedback that's pertinent to the project or task at hand. Avoid bringing up unrelated issues or past mistakes.

- **Balance positive and constructive feedback:** Starting with positive feedback can open a receptive channel for constructive feedback. This approach is often referred to as the 'sandwich' method.

- **Avoid personal criticism:** Focus on the work, not the person. Comments should be about behaviour or performance, not personal attributes.

- **Be timely:** Provide feedback soon after the event or behaviour, so it's fresh and relevant.

- **Encourage dialogue:** After offering feedback, allow the recipient to share their perspective. This can foster understanding and collaboration.

- **Stay calm and objective:** Especially if the feedback is critical, deliver it without showing signs of frustration or anger.

And here are some tips for receiving feedback:

- **Listen actively:** Pay attention to what's being said without immediately reacting. Understand the core of the feedback before responding.

- **Ask for clarification:** If you're unsure about a point being made, ask for specific examples or further explanation.

- **Thank the giver:** Even if the feedback is tough to hear, expressing gratitude for the feedback can foster a positive environment.

- **Separate self from work:** Remember that feedback is about your work or behaviour, not your worth as a person.

- **Reflect and analyse:** After receiving feedback, take some time to consider its validity and usefulness. Not all feedback may be applicable, but reflecting allows you to discern what's valuable.

- **Seek feedback proactively:** Regularly ask for feedback to understand areas of improvement and strengths. This proactive approach can help you grow faster and align better with the project's goals.

- **Avoid being defensive:** While it's natural to want to defend your actions, it's more productive to listen, understand the other person's perspective and then explain if necessary.

- **Act on feedback:** If the feedback is valid and actionable, make the necessary changes. This demonstrates your commitment to growth and continuous improvement.

Remember, feedback is a tool for growth. When given and received effectively, it fosters personal development, strengthens team dynamics and drives project success.

# Practice Leadership Reflection

Remember, the five ingredients of practice leadership are: **decision making, team building, communication, delegation,** and **performance management**.

Here are five questions I encourage you to reflect on. Think of a project or situation you have experienced and note the behaviours and actions back then. Now after reading about practice leadership how would you approach a similar project or situation next time.

1.  How do you approach decision making in complex scenarios?

2.  How do you motivate your team members?

3.  How effective are your communication skills?

4.  How do you delegate tasks within your team?

5.  How often do you provide feedback?

# Practice Leadership Checklist

Use this checklist to track over time how you have developed your practice leadership strengths. Tick what you are consistently doing well and select three you are going to focus on next.

- o  I make informed decisions, even under pressure.
- o  I have a cohesive and motivated team.
- o  I communicate clearly and effectively.
- o  I delegate tasks appropriately.
- o  I provide regular feedback to my team members.
- o  I am comfortable leading change and can manage the associated uncertainty.
- o  I communicate my vision and goals clearly to my team.
- o  I am adept at maintaining the motivation and morale of my team.
- o  I can evaluate the success of a project and identify areas of improvement.
- o  I foster an environment where team members feel empowered and responsible.

- I regularly check in with team members to assess progress and provide support.

- I promote a collaborative environment where every team member feels valued.

- I can step in and provide direct help when necessary.

- I ensure that project objectives align with broader organisational goals.

- I openly celebrate successes and view failures as learning opportunities.

- I maintain an open dialogue with stakeholders, managing their expectations and keeping them informed.

# The Secret Sauce for Lasting Success

Well done — you made it through all fifteen ingredients that shape real project leadership: self leadership, solution leadership and practice leadership.

At the very start of this book, you heard about three project team leaders — Andrea, Henry and Lily — all of whom were struggling in their roles due to a range of problems. Now I'd like you to hear from some other project team leaders who also faced significant challenges, and potentially huge fallouts, but were able to turn things around and come out stronger...

Adrian was assigned to lead a high-profile project in his organisation. Despite his extensive experience, the thought of failure scared him. He feared the potential blow his reputation would take if the project failed. Over time, he realised that reputation was built not only on success but also on how one handles failure. With a new perspective, he openly communicated potential risks to stakeholders and effectively managed expectations, protecting his reputation in the process.

Susan had recently been promoted and was assigned to manage a highly technical project. The fear of appearing incompetent because of her lack of technical knowledge haunted her. One day, she decided to rely on her leadership skills. She organised a meeting with her team and openly shared her concern, emphasising that everyone's expertise was important. The team appreciated her honesty and dedication, viewing her not as incompetent but as an effective and humble leader.

John was leading a complex, costly project. The fear of budget and time blowouts was always lurking in his mind. John decided to adopt rigorous project management tools and involve his team in creating a realistic, detailed plan. As the project advanced, there were still some unexpected challenges, but John's proactive approach minimised the impact and helped control both the budget and timeline, easing his fear.

Mary, who prided herself on leading transformative projects, was assigned to a project that, at face value, appeared to be merely maintaining the status quo. She feared not making a significant impact or difference. Over time, Mary realised that every project has potential for impact, and decided to focus on improving internal processes and team culture. Her efforts significantly improved team morale and efficiency, making a lasting impact that assuaged her fear.

Robert was tasked with overseeing a multi-dimensional project that seemed chaotic from the onset. The fear of getting lost in the chaos was overwhelming. He decided to break the project down into manageable parts, and assigned clear roles and responsibilities. As he began to see order emerging from the chaos, his fear gradually diminished. He learned that being lost is temporary and often a precursor to finding a clearer path.

What do all of these project team leaders have in common? They utilised the Real Project Leadership model to address specific challenges within their work and help their project teams achieve *real* impact. And now you have an opportunity to do the same.

It is up to you to make and taste the **Real Project Leadership** recipe. Like a chef who will try recipes over and over again to create that magical dish, it's all about perfecting the recipe through repetition and consistency. The more a chef tries a recipe, the better they become at it. They learn how to adjust the ingredients, cooking time and temperature to achieve the desired taste and texture.

But before you go, I want to share two final concepts with you: role model and team legacy. You can think of these as the secret sauce of the Real Project Leadership recipe, ensuring lasting success for you and your team.

# Role model

Is there someone in your organisation, network or team you talk about often as having an influence on you? Or someone you look to for inspiration or guidance?

'Your own actions are a better reflection of you than any words you can ever speak.'

– Malala Yousafzai, activist, author and
2014 Nobel Peace Prize laureate

By understanding the differences between good and bad role models, each project team member – project sponsors, project managers, business analysts, change analysts, subject matter experts, developers and testers – can strive to embody the qualities of a good role model. This collective project leadership effort can significantly enhance team dynamics, performance and overall project success.

Project teams bring together several people to plan and deliver change. Some are experienced project professionals, some are subject matter experts, and some are taking a leap into an unknown workspace. One thing they all have in common is the **choice to be a good or bad role model**.

Here is a story about an organisation investing in strategic change to modernise the workplace and stay competitive in an ever-changing digital landscape. The two project managers, Sarah and Tom, had different teams working on this massive program of work.

Sarah was a shining example of a good role model. She was empathetic, always making an effort to understand her team members' needs and concerns. She was known for her excellent communication skills, which helped her articulate project goals and expectations clearly. Sarah also had a strong sense of accountability and integrity, taking responsibility for her actions and decisions while fostering a culture of ownership within her team.

Sarah's team thrived. They were motivated, engaged and committed to the project's success. They appreciated Sarah's transparency, which built trust among team members. Sarah's ability to adapt and respond effectively to setbacks allowed her team to navigate challenges with resilience. She encouraged a continuous learning mindset and, as a result, her team members were always eager to develop their skills and share their knowledge with one another.

On the other hand, Tom was a prime example of a bad role model. He was often distant and unapproachable, making it difficult for his team members to communicate with him. Tom's lack of emotional intelligence led to misunderstandings and conflicts within the team. He often delegated tasks without providing clear instructions or expectations, leading to confusion and inefficiencies.

Tom's lack of accountability and integrity resulted in a blame-oriented culture within his team. Whenever there was an issue or setback, Tom would quickly assign blame to someone else instead of taking responsibility and finding a solution. This behaviour fostered a toxic work environment, causing team members to become disengaged and demotivated.

As the digital transformation program progressed, it became increasingly apparent that Sarah's team was achieving milestones on time and within budget, while Tom's team struggled to keep up. The contrast in team dynamics and performance caught the attention of the executive sponsor, who decided to intervene.

They organised a series of workshops and coaching sessions for Tom to help him improve his leadership skills and become a better role model for his team. They also assigned a mentor to work closely with Tom, guiding him on his journey to become a more effective leader.

Over time, Tom began to understand the importance of being a good role model. He started to practise active listening, empathy and clear communication. He embraced accountability and worked towards fostering a culture of ownership within his team. Gradually, Tom's team began to show signs of improvement, and their performance started to catch up with that of Sarah's team.

The story of Sarah and Tom serves as a reminder that the impact of being a good role model cannot be underestimated in a project environment.

Good role models can inspire their teams to overcome challenges, learn and grow together, ultimately leading to project success. On the other hand, bad role models can hinder progress and create a toxic environment, jeopardising the project's results. It is crucial for **all project team members to embody the qualities of a good role model**, and continuously strive to improve their project leadership skills to ensure the success of their teams and projects.

# Team legacy

Ever thought about the lasting impact your project team is creating?

In a relay race, each runner passes the baton to the next, with every athlete contributing to the outcome. A team's legacy is like that baton, carrying the collective efforts, values and achievements of one generation to the next, ensuring that the race continues, and the spirit of teamwork endures.

# Every project is more than just a task – it's a legacy in the making!

In a rapidly evolving business landscape, projects have become more than just assignments with a start and end date. They have transformed into powerful vehicles that allow teams to etch their mark and leave behind a legacy. For those in project and change management roles, recognising this potential not only elevates the impact of the work but also inspires project teams to strive for excellence. Here are six key points to consider:

- **Projects as building blocks for tomorrow:** Each project an organisation undertakes is a brick in the foundation of its future. Whether it's a small initiative to improve internal processes or a massive endeavour to launch a groundbreaking product, each project contributes to the organisation's narrative. These narratives, over time, culminate in the legacy that the organisation leaves for future generations. They become the milestones that future teams look back on for inspiration, guidance and motivation.

- **Showcasing innovation and expertise:** Projects provide an opportunity for teams to showcase their innovative spirit and expertise. The solutions developed, methodologies adopted, and results achieved become a testament to the team's capabilities. They set the benchmark for what's possible, and inspire others within and outside the organisation to push boundaries.

- **Creating stories of resilience and triumph:** All projects will experience challenges – unexpected roadblocks, resource constraints, or shifting priorities. How a team navigates these challenges, adapts to changes, and still delivers successful outcomes creates stories of resilience and triumph. These stories serve as lessons for future teams facing similar challenges.

- **Driving cultural change and evolution:** Change has the power to shape and redefine the cultural fabric of an organisation. This might involve introducing new technologies, processes or behaviours. By successfully managing and leading these projects, teams play a pivotal role in influencing how the organisation evolves, how it operates and what it values. This influence, in turn, leaves a lasting imprint on the organisation's identity.

- **Offering tangible value beyond completion:** A well-executed project often results in tangible assets – be it intellectual property, a strengthened brand image, or new revenue streams. These assets continue to provide value long after the project's completion, ensuring that the team's efforts are recognised and remembered. They serve as a legacy of the team's ability to create enduring value for the organisation.

- **Empowering and inspiring future teams:** One of the most profound ways projects leave a legacy is by serving as a learning tool for future teams. Documented experiences, retrospectives and lessons learned become invaluable resources. They empower future project managers and teams with insights, helping them avoid pitfalls and capitalise on what has worked in the past.

For those leading and managing projects, it's essential to instil a 'legacy mindset' within your teams. Here's how:

- **Visionary thinking:** Encourage your team to see beyond the immediate deliverables. How will this project impact the organisation in three, five or ten years?

- **Documenting and reflecting:** Make it a habit to document experiences, successes and failures. This documentation isn't just for review; it's a legacy in the making.

- **Celebrating and recognising:** Celebrate the completion of projects, not just for meeting objectives but for the lasting impact they're bound to create.

- **Continuous learning:** Promote a culture where past projects are studied, and lessons are drawn. Ensure that knowledge transfer is integral to your project processes.

Projects are more than tasks and timelines; they're opportunities. Opportunities to innovate, to shape the future, to inspire and to leave a legacy. As you embark on your next project, take a moment to reflect. Ask yourself:

How will this project be remembered?

What legacy will it leave behind?

Every project, no matter how big or small, has the potential to leave a lasting mark. Embrace that potential and let it guide your journey.

# References

1. https://www.weforum.org/publications/the-future-of-jobs-report-2023/digest

2. https://hbr.org/2023/10/4-forces-that-are-fundamentally-changing-how-we-work

3. https://www.gartner.com/en/newsroom/press-releases/2022-10-24-gartner-hr-research-identifies-new-framework-for-organizations-to-succeed-in-todays-fragmented-workplace

4. https://www.cio.com/article/230427/why-it-projects-still-fail.html

5. https://hbr.org/2017/01/the-neuroscience-of-trust

6. https://hbr.org/2021/05/high-performing-teams-start-with-a-culture-of-shared-values

7. https://repository.lboro.ac.uk/articles/thesis/Resilience_in_projects_definition_dimensions_antecedents_and_consequences/9454760

8. https://dictionary.cambridge.org/dictionary/english/self-discipline

9. https://www.weforum.org/agenda/2020/10/top-10-work-skills-of-tomorrow-how-long-it-takes-to-learn-them/

10. https://www.mckinsey.com/featured-insights/future-of-work/retraining-and-reskilling-workers-in-the-age-of-automation

11. https://www.pmi.org/about/press-media/press-releases/2018-pulse-of-the-profession-survey#:~:text=The%20study%20shows%20that%20on,are%20not%20completed%20on%20time

12. https://www.mckinsey.com/capabilities/people-and-organizational-performance/our-insights/decision-making-in-the-age-of-urgency

13. https://expertprogrammanagement.com/2017/09/decision-matrix-analysis/

14. https://www.gallup.com/workplace/312683/lead-remote-team-away-burnout-not-toward.aspx

15. https://teambuilding.com/blog/team-building-statistics#:~:text=Per%20capita%2C%20Singapore%20shows%20a,order%20of%20interest%20per%20capita.&text=Want%20our%20best%20tips%20for%20building%20happier%20teams%3F

# About Jeanette

Hello, you can call me JC. My first name, Jeanette, is also my mother's middle name.

My girls, daughter Kirsty and granddaughter Willow, are my inspiration, my why.

I am curious and learn every day. I love chocolate.

I cheer loud and proud as a Gold Coast Suns AFL Club Foundation Member.

Did I mention I love facilitating workshops? It is my happy place.

Growing up on a farm in country Queensland, every day there was a job to do — before school, after school and on the weekends. No complaints, life was simple.

Maths and science were my favourite subjects at school. From as early as I can remember, I wanted to be a school teacher but that is not what played out.

I spent more than twenty-five years leading large projects in government, education and utility sectors, working as a logistics

officer, contracts administrator, PMO coordinator, project manager and program director. This provided development opportunities to strengthen my skills and knowledge about real project leadership. I didn't start off thinking, 'I am going to be a project professional', but with my curiosity and appetite to learn I continuously put up my hand for the next challenge.

That said, the most impactful learning I had about leadership and teamwork was in the sporting arena. I was privileged to be part of AFL participation and talent programs for twenty years.

In 2017, based on hundreds of hours of interviews and research, and unpacking all of my own project case studies, I developed **The Project Ecosystem**® – a planning and delivery framework. This framework is the basis of all my programs and workshops.

This was the start of my practice.

I now help organisations with their business transformation journeys, integrating customer, product, process, technology and leadership capabilities.

You'll find me advising, facilitating, training or coaching with:

- **General managers and directors** who are dealing with poor customer satisfaction ratings, struggling to get staff to adopt new ways of working, noticing financial leakage in their budget reports, and are frustrated with out-of-date systems and broken processes, yet are accountable for program performance results.

- **Project teams** who have competing priorities, scope changes, capacity challenges, and stakeholder engagement and communication issues, yet are responsible for delivering on time and budget.

I would love to work with you and your teams. My program Accelerate and one day workshops are based on one or more of the ingredients from the proven recipe you have read in this book.

Find more information on my website: https://jeanettecremor.com.au/accelerate/

Let's chat about what is on your mind or how you are using the **Real Project Leadership** ingredients and secret sauce.

Sign up to my newsletter https://www.jeanettecremor.com.au/sign-up/

Connect with me on LinkedIn: https://www.linkedin.com/in/jeanettemcremor

Send me an email jc@jeanettecremor.com.au

www.ingramcontent.com/pod-product-compliance
Lightning Source LLC
Chambersburg PA
CBHW071643210326
41597CB00017B/2099